· 汉英对照 ·

中国历代笑话精选(三)

Selected Jokes From Past Chinese Dynasties (Ⅲ)

陈懿 编注 于岑 翻译

刘峰 刘耕涛 绘图

华语教学出版社

北　京

SINOLINGUA BEIJING

First Edition	1997
Second Printing	2000
Third Printing	2002

ISBN 7-80052-509-0

Copyright 2002 by Sinolingua

Published by Sinolingua

24 Baiwanzhuang Road, Beijing 100037, China

Tel: (86) 10-68995871 / 68326333

Fax: (86) 10-68326333

E-mail: sinolingua@ihw.com.cn

Printed by Beijing Foreign Languages Printing House

Distributed by China International

Book Trading Corporation

35 Chegongzhuang Xilu, P.O. Box 399

Beijing 100044, China

Printed in the People's Republic of China

出版者的话

生活离不开笑话,笑话也离不开生活。

数千年来,勤劳智慧的中国人民在创造了灿烂的古代文明的同时,给后人留下了又一笔丰厚的文化遗产——数以万计的历代笑话。它们或幽默,或讽刺,或诙谐,或辛辣;它们针砭流弊,讥讽陋习,启迪借鉴,弃恶扬善。它们植根于广阔的社会生活,因此枝叶繁茂,历久不衰。

今天我们从这些笑话中精选了数百篇,对文字内容进行了疏通修改,略加注释,配以插图,并附有英译文,辑为若干册,每册百篇左右,奉献给喜爱并希望了解中国历代笑话的中外读者,愿朋友们在笑声中多有收获。

Publisher's Note

Take jokes away from life and you take a good part of life away from man. Throughout China's history the industrious and ingenious Chinese people, while creating a brilliant ancient civilization, have left succeeding generations a rich cultural heritage of tens of thousands of jokes, spanning many different dynasties. The jokes are humorous, sarcastic, witty, and pointed. They unmask corrupt and evil practices, ridicule the ugly and ignorant, and are generally relieving as well as enlightening. Rooted in society at large, they flourish and will always be with us.

We have selected several hundred well-known jokes and added footnotes, illustrations and English translations. Each of the several volumes contains around a hundred jokes. The book is dedicated to international readers interested in China and its people. We hope these jokes from past Chinese dynasties will offer many amusing insights into the character of the Chinese people.

前　言

人需要幽默和欢笑，因为生活中既有明媚的春天，热烈的夏天，斑斓的秋天，也有凛冽的冬天。笑，是友爱的伴侣、健康的朋友、奋进的动力。会心的微笑、舒怀的大笑、轻蔑的冷笑，都能给人启迪：否定和嘲讽假恶丑，肯定和颂扬真善美。

笑话在我国典籍里出现得相当早，在先秦诸子散文和历史散文中就已经引用流传于民间的短小的笑话，来说明某一个道理。这些由劳动人民口头创作，依靠人民群众口耳相传的笑话，体现了世世代代劳动人民的生活感触和情绪倾向，闪烁着劳动人民的诙谐幽默和机智聪明之光。古代笑话无论是在思想内容上，还是在艺术手法上，都有着杰出的成就。它们丰富而深刻的思想内容，既为我们提供了认识社会的生动材料，又给我们以思想方法和工作方法上的各种启示；在艺术上为我们今天笑的艺术创作提供了可资借鉴的宝贵经验。

本集收入历代笑话九十九篇。读者将通过本书笑话中对无知的嘲讽，对愚昧的讥刺，对虚伪的揭露，对丑恶的鞭挞，多侧面地了解历史，理解今天，增强辨别真善美和假恶丑的能力，提高逻辑思维能力，学会运用语言艺术幽默地表现丰富多彩的生活。

Preface

Man needs humor and laughter just as nature is endowed with the four seasons. Laughter accompanies friends and health, and always elevates man's spirit. An understanding laugh, a happy laugh and a contemptuous laugh — each has a message, whether it is to ridicule and rebuke the false, evil and ugly, or to appreciate and praise the true, kind and beautiful.

Jokes appeared as early as 3,000 years ago in ancient Chinese records and prose writings as short, funny stories to illustrate a point of truth. These folk anecdotes were circulated and handed down from mouth to mouth, reflecting the experiences and sentiments of the people and sparkling with their resourcefulness and humor. They are remarkable either as folk literature or as an art — rich, deep and enlightening, a precious legacy for today's culture of laughter.

This bilingual illustrated book includes 99 jokes selected from a tradition which is centuries old. Some satirize ignorance and meanness, and some expose hypocrisy and evil. They should make interesting reading for international students of the Chinese language who, while learning more of the language and savoring the humor, will gain an insight into Chinese ethics and folk philosophy, and be better able to understand Chinese people today.

目　录

I

CONTENTS

1. 多亏了这顶毡帽①

有个人在烈日炎炎的盛夏戴着一顶毡帽赶路，没走出一里远，就热得满头大汗。他见路旁有一棵大树，便走到树下去歇凉②，并顺手摘下毡帽当作扇子扇起来。他一边扇，一边自言自语："今儿个多亏了这顶毡帽，要不然，就把我给热死了！"

① 毡帽：用羊毛或其他动物毛经湿、热、挤压而成的片状 物制成的帽子，具有良好的保温作用。北方人用以御寒。A kind of felt hat worn in North China.

② 歇凉：北方方言，即乘凉。(Northern dialect) relax in a cool place.

1. Thanks to the Felt Hat

A man wearing a felt hat was travelling on a hot summer day. Before long, he was bathed in sweat. Seeing a big tree by the roadside, he went over and sat in its shade. He took off his felt hat and fanned himself with it, murmuring: "Lucky I've got my felt hat on today. Otherwise, I would have perished from heat."

2. 千手观音①

　　有个人初学剃头②,每剃破一处,就用一根手指按住。后来,伤口越来越多,十个手指怎么也按不过来。他心急火燎③。最后,干脆把剃头刀往地上一扔,喟然长叹④道:"原来剃头也这么难,非得是千手观音才行啊!"

---

　　① 千手观音:佛教大乘菩萨之一。《大藏经》有《金刚智》译本,中有观音图像,体具千臂。千手观音即本于此。A Budhisattva (Avalokitesvara) with 1,000 hands.
　　② 剃头:用刀刮去头发。Shave the head.
　　③ 心急火燎(liǎo):心里着急,犹如火烧一般。Burning with frustration.
　　④ 喟(kuì)然长叹:因感慨而叹息。Heave a deep sigh.

2. Thousand-Handed Avalokitesvara

A young barber started to shave the head of his first customer. Each time he made a mistake and cut the customer's head he would cover the wound with his finger. Later, as there were more and more cuts, he just couldn't cover all of them even though he used all his fingers. Finally in great frustration, he threw the razor onto the ground and sighed deeply: "Oh, I didn't know that this was a job that only the thousand-handed Avalokitesvara could do!"

3. 没有朝下长的树杈

乡村里的凳子,大多是用现成的树杈子做腿的。有一家的凳腿坏了,父亲叫儿子到山里找一个树杈子来修理。儿子拿着斧子就出了门。

整整一天过去了,儿子才空着手回来。父亲生气地责骂他。他理直气壮地分辩道:"这能怪我吗?山里的树杈子全是朝上长的。我找了一天,也没找到一个朝下长的。"

3. No Forked Branches
Grow Downward

In a certain village the stool legs were mostly made from forked tree branches. One day a man told his son to go and chop a new forked branch to replace the broken one for a stool. The son went out with an ax. A whole day passed and he came back empty handed.

The father was annoyed, but the son retorted with perfect assurance: "How can you blame me? All the forked branches are growing upward. I searched all day but I just couldn't find one that was growing downward!"

4. 止风药

有一次,和尚①、道士②和医生三个人一起坐船过河。船到河中心,突然起了大风,风急浪高,把船颠得忽上忽下,随时都有翻沉的危险。

这时,船家恳求和尚和道士说:"两位先生都是出门修行③之人,请你们祈神止风如何?"于是和尚祷告说:"念彼观音④力,风浪尽平息!"道士跟着祷告:"风伯⑤雨师⑥,各安方位,急急如律令⑦!"

和尚、道士刚祷告完,医生也在嘟嘟囔囔:"荆芥、薄荷、金银花、苦楝子!"

船家听见后不解地问他:"您这位先生数说⑧这些药名又是为什么呢?"

医生一本正经地回答说:"我这几味药,都是止风⑨的!"

---

① 和尚:指出家修行的男佛教徒。Buddhist monk.
② 道士:道教的教徒。Daoist priest.
③ 修行:佛教称出家为修行。(Buddhist term) practice religion.
④ 观音:佛教大乘菩萨之一,亦称观世音。(Buddhism) The Goddess of Mercy, or Avalokitesvara.
⑤ 风伯:即风神。The God of Wind.
⑥ 雨师:司雨之神。The God of Rain.
⑦ 急急如律令:道家用于符咒之末的套语。马上照办。(Daoist incantation) please do it at once.
⑧ 数说:逐一叙说。Recite one by one.
⑨ 风:中医指某些疾病,如羊痫风等。和风雨的风,同字不同义。A Chinese medical term for diseases such as epilepsy. It is a homophone of 风 (wind).

4. Wind-Dispelling Medicine

One day a Buddhist monk, a Daoist priest and a doctor were crossing a river together in a boat. Just as they reached the middle of the river, there suddenly arose a strong wind. The waves surged with the rising wind, so the boat was tossed up and down and seemed about to capsize at any minute.

8

Then the boatman begged the Buddhist monk and the Daoist priest: "Since you two gentlemen practice religion, would you please pray to the Gods to stop the wind?" The Buddhist monk chanted: "Almighty Avalokitesvara, I pray that you will use your great power to stop the waves and wind!" The Daoist priest also prayed: "Ye Gods of Wind and Rain, please restore calm."

When they had finished praying, the doctor chimed in with: "Schizonepeta, peppermint, honeysuckle, chinaberry..."

The puzzled boatman asked: "Why are you reciting the names of medicines, sir?" The doctor replied earnestly: "Wella, you see, those medicines are all good for dispelling wind."

5. 买奴

从前有个村庄,村里有个财主,一家人都有些呆。一天,财主让儿子去市场买个奴仆,临行前一再嘱咐:"要少花钱买个好的。"

儿子来到市场,从铜镜商店经过,从陈列着的铜镜中看到自己的影子,觉得又年青又健壮。于是心中暗想:这一定是市场上要卖的好奴仆。便指着镜子问道:"这个奴仆要卖多少钱?"卖镜子的人看出他是个呆子,便骗他道:"这个奴仆只要一万钱①。"他觉得不贵,便付钱买了镜子,揣到怀里回家去了。

到了家,老财主问他:"你买的奴仆在哪儿?"

"在我怀里。"

"快取出来让我看看好不好。"

老财主拿过镜子一看,只见镜中人须眉皓首,面目黑皱,不觉大怒,骂道:"哪有用一万钱,买这么一个老奴的!"举起手杖要打儿子。

儿子吓得跑去向母亲求救。母亲抱着小女儿赶快走来,对老财主说:"先别着急,让我来看看。"她看了看镜子,嗔怪丈夫道:"呆老头子,我儿子只用一万钱,就买了母女两奴婢,你怎么还嫌贵呢!"

老财主听了很高兴。

5. Buying a Servant

Once there was a rich old man in a village. Everyone in his family was somewhat muddle-headed. One day the rich man told his son to go and buy a servant in the market, telling him time and again before he set out: "Choose a good one and spend as little money as possible."

---

① 钱:货币。Ancient Chinese currency.

The son went to the market where he passed a bronze-mirror shop. He saw in one of the mirrors his own reflection. The person in the mirror was young and strong, so he felt that this must be a good worker for sale. So, pointing at the mirror, he asked the shopkeeper: "How much to buy this servant?" The shopkeeper saw that he was an idiot and said: "This servant can be bought for only 10,000 *qian*." The young man thought it was not expensive, so he bought the mirror and took it home with him.

When he got home, his father asked, "Where's the servant you bought?"

"Inside my coat."

"Take him out and let me have a look."

The rich old man looked in the mirror and saw a wrinkled face with a white beard and eyebrows. He flew into a rage and scolded his son: "How can you spend 10,000 *qian* on such a broken-down old man?" As he said this, he raised his stick to beat his son.

The son was scared and ran to his mother for help. The mother, with a little baby girl in her arms, hurried over and said: "Let me have a look."

She looked in the mirror and then turned to berate her husband: "You stupid old man! Our son has bought two servants, a mother and daughter, for only 10,000 *qian*. How can you call that expensive?"

Thereupon, the rich old man became pleased.

6. 煮床席①

三国②时,一个蜀国人到吴国。吴国人设宴款待,其中有一盘是竹笋③。蜀人觉得很好吃,便问是什么东西。吴人告诉他:"这是竹子。"

---

① 床席:这里指用竹篾编成的片状物,供坐卧铺垫的用具。A kind of mat made of thin bamboo strips used as a seat cover or bedspread.

② 三国:中国朝代名,公元220年起到280年止,其时魏国、蜀国、吴国鼎立。The Three Kingdoms Period (220－280), during which the State of Wei, the State of Shu and the State of Wu confronted one another.

③ 竹笋:竹子的嫩茎、芽,出产于中国南方,有的可供食用,味鲜美。Bamboo shoots, edible and tasty, grow mostly in southern China.

蜀人回到家后,就把铺在床上的竹席剁①碎了,放在锅里来煮,煮了好久,总是煮不熟,他怒冲冲地对妻子说道:"吴人心眼真鬼②,竟如此骗我!"

6. Cooking the Bamboo Mat

During the Three Kingdoms Period a man from the State of Shu went to the State of Wu and was treated to a banquet. Among the dishes there was one made of bamboo shoots. The man ate it with great relish and asked what it was. The people there told him:"This is bamboo."

After he got home he chopped the bamboo mat on his bed to pieces and boiled it in a pot. But no matter how long he boiled it, it was never done. He said to his wife furiously:"Those wicked Wu scoundrels told me a lie!"

---

① 剁(duò):斫,斩碎。Chop.
② 鬼:喻称人心的阴险、狡诈或不光明。Insidious, crafty.

15

7. 疑姓

某县县令①老婆姓伍,有一天她会见县衙门②中各官的眷属③。

县令老婆首先问县丞老婆姓什么,回答说:"姓陆。"又问主簿老婆,回答说:"姓戚。"县令老婆听后勃然大怒④,转身回到自己房间。这几位眷属也不知什么原因,只好都愣⑤在那儿。

县令听说后,赶快进屋问是怎么回事。县令老婆说:"我问他们姓什么,一个说姓陆,一个说姓戚,这都是因为我姓伍所以才故意这么说⑥。如果我再问别人,不说姓八姓九才怪⑦呢!"

---

① 县令:一县的行政长官。County magistrate.
② 衙门:旧时官署的名称。Name of government office in the old days.
③ 眷属:家属,亲属。这里指县官的夫人。Family dependents, relatives; (here) county officials' wives.
④ 勃然大怒:因发怒而变脸色的样子。Flare up, flush with rage.
⑤ 愣(lèng):呆,失神的样子。Dumbfounded, look blankly.
⑥ 陆:中文中六的大写。戚(qī):在中文中和七同音;伍:中文中五的大写;六、七都比五大,所以县令老婆不高兴。陆, capital form of the number six. 戚, a homonym of seven. 伍, capital form of the number five. As seven and six are bigger than five, the magistrate's wife was upset.
⑦ 怪:惊异,奇怪。Find something strange; be surprised at.

7. Suspicious Names

A county magistrate's wife surnamed Wu one day interviewed the wives of all the county officials. The magistrate's wife first asked the name of the deputy magistrate's wife and was told "Lu". She then asked the woman whose husband was the chief secretary, and the answer was "Qi". The magistrate's wife was very upset and stalked away to her private room. Baffled, the officials' wives stood there not knowing what to say.

When the magistrate heard about this, he hurried over to inquire what the matter was. His wife said: "I asked their surnames. One said 'Lu', another said 'Qi'. They must have said it on purpose because they know my surname is Wu. If I go on asking, I bet the next two will say they're surnamed 'Ba' and 'Jiu'".

8. 家里出了贞妇①

有个秀才②既呆又多疑。

有一天,他在家悄悄躲到暗处。等妻子走过的时候,他突然窜出来上前搂抱。妻子大吃一惊,一面挣

_____

① 贞妇:指丈夫死后不另嫁的妇女。A woman who refused to re-marry after her husband's death.

② 秀才:中国明清两代称通过最低一级科举考试的读书人。A scholar who had passed the lowest level of the imperial examination during the Ming and Qing dynasties.

扎，一面破口大骂①。这秀才便高兴地说："我们家出了一个贞妇了！"

8. There's a Chaste Woman in Our Family

There was once a scholar who was both stupid and suspicious. Once he hid himself in the dark. As his wife passed by he suddenly jumped out and hugged her. His wife was terribly alarmed and struggled desperately while bursting into abuse.

The scholar said, very pleased: "There's a chaste woman in our family."

---

① 破口大骂：凶狠恶毒地怒骂。Curse viciously.

9. 与秦桧①通奸

有一个秀才读史书,看到令人不平的地方,一定咬牙切齿②,拍着桌子怒骂不止。这一天,他读到秦桧害死岳飞③父子的事,不觉怒火万丈④,拍着桌子大骂。他妻子在旁劝道:"家里只有十张桌子,你已经拍碎九张了,留下这张桌子我们吃饭用吧!"秀才转脸怒叱⑤道:"是不是你与秦桧通奸呢?"于是把妻子痛打了一顿。

9. A Liaison With Qin Hui

There was once a scholar who, whenever he read about a case of injustice in a history book,

---

① 秦桧(huì)(1090—1155)。南宋投降派代表人物,曾两任宰相,前后执政十九年,杀害抗金名将岳飞父子,为人民所痛恨。Qin Hui (1090—1155), head of a capitulationist clique of the Southern Song Dynasty, twice prime minister, in power for 19 years; notorious for murdering Yue Fei and his son.

② 咬牙切齿:形容痛恨到极点的样子。Hate most bitterly.

③ 岳飞(1103—1142):南宋抗金名将,多次大败金军,后被诬谋反,与其子岳云、部将张宪同被杀害。Yue Fei (1103—1142), a famous general of the Southern Song Dynasty. He repeatedly beat the invading Jin troops but was falsely accused of plotting a rebellion, and was murdered together with his son Yue Yun and his subordinate Zhang Xian.

④ 怒火万丈:怒火,指强烈的愤怒;万丈,极言愤怒强烈的程度。怒火, great indignation; 万丈, to the highest degree.

⑤ 叱(chi):大声责骂。Rebuke loudly.

would gnash his teeth, smite the table and give vent to a storm of abuse. One day, when he was reading the story of Yue Fei and his son being murdered by Qin Hui, he was filled with indignation and again flew into a rage. When his wife pleaded with him: "We have ten tables in the house and you've broken nine. Please save this one so we can have our meals on it," the scholar yelled, "I bet you had a liaison with Qin Hui, didn't you?" Then he gave his wife a good beating.

10. 束脩①被晒化了

昆山②人周用斋,傻气十足。

一次,他在别人那里教书,看到主人在黄梅季节③把衣服等东西来晾晒,也连忙回到房中把书袋及主人给的束脩一起拿出来晾晒,结果被人趁机偷走了一些。等他再来看时,心里嘀咕④起来:"怎么会少了呢?"他的学生告诉他说:"那是被太阳晒化⑤了。"

10. Melting Meat

Zhou Yongzhai, although a teacher, was a blockhead.

Once, when he served as a tutor in someone's home, he saw that his master had his clothes aired

---

① 束脩:脩为干肉,十条干肉为束脩。这里指学生以干肉给教师致送的报酬。脩 is cured meat. Ten pieces of cured meat is 束脩, which means here the payment for the tutor.

② 昆山:县名,属江苏省。Name of a county in what is now Jiangsu Province.

③ 黄梅季节:夏初梅子黄熟之时,江淮流域常阴雨连绵,比较潮湿,俗称黄梅。The plum season is in early summer, when the plums turn yellow and ripen

④ 嘀咕:私下说,小声说。Have misgivings about something.

⑤ 化:熔化,溶化。Melt.

23

in the sun because it was the plum season. He hurried to his room and took out the cured meat which was his salary and put it to dry in the sun too. While he was away somebody stole some of the meat, and when the scholar returned he exclaimed: "There seems to be less meat now than there was before." His student told him: "It has been melted by the sun."

11. 下水船①

　　有一次一个人乘船上行②,他看到迎面而来的船犹如脱缰之马③、离弦之箭④,急速驶过,心里十分奇怪,便问船夫:"这是什么船?"船夫回答说:"这是下水船。"他听后大笑说:"造船的人多笨呀!如果都造下水船,难道不好吗?"

---

　　① 下水船:顺流而下的船。Downstream boat.
　　② 上行:船逆水而上。Upstream boat.
　　③ 脱缰之马:像脱离了缰绳的马,比喻行动迅速。A runaway horse; describing a very fast speed.
　　④ 离弦之箭:已射出的箭,比喻行动快捷。An arrow discharged from the bowstring; a very swift action.

11. Downstream Boat

Once a man was taking an upstream boat. He saw that the boats sailing toward him were moving as fast as horses running wild or even arrows shot from bows. He asked his boatman: "What kind of boats are those?" The boatman answered: "They're downstream boats." Upon hearing this, the man gave a loud laugh and said: "How stupid the boat builders are! Wouldn't it be better if they made all their boats downstream boats!"

12. 吃河豚^①

从前有一对夫妻,在集市上买了几斤河豚,准备炖^②着吃。

河豚炖熟以后,因为害怕有毒,夫妻俩谁也不敢先吃,于是互相推让起来。

---

① 河豚:鱼的一种,肉味鲜美,唯卵巢、血液和肝脏有剧毒,处理不当,人吃后会中毒,以致死亡。Globefish, with delicious meat but toxic ovaries, blood and liver. It is poisonous when not properly prepared.

② 炖:和汤煮烂食物。Stew.

后来，妻子不得已，只好拿起筷子先吃。她一边用筷子去夹河豚肉，一边痛哭流涕地对丈夫说："我先吃了，万一有个三长两短①，我只求你看管好咱们的两个儿女，等他们长大了，千万不要再买河豚吃。"

12. Eating Globefish

Once there was a couple who bought a few *jin* of globefish from the market and stewed it.

When the fish was done, they urged each other to eat first, because they were afraid it might be poisonous.

Finally, the wife took up the chopsticks first. While picking up the fish, she wept bitterly and said to her husband："I'll try it first. If anything should happen to me, I just beg you to take good care of our two children. Tell them when they grow up never to buy globefish."

---

① 三长两短：指意外的灾祸、事故，多指人的死亡。Unexpected disaster or accident, especially death.

13. 怪你昨日不送客

有一天，迂公①请了几个朋友来家里喝酒。喝到八九成②时，迂公趴③在桌子上睡着了。

迂公睡醒以后，误以为已经过了一夜。他睁开眼看见满座的朋友，便瞪④着眼珠子问道："今儿个⑤我没有给大家下帖，诸位怎么又都来了呢？"

---

① 迂(yū)公：指拘泥守旧、不明事理的人。A pedant or stickler for formalities; somebody lacking in common sense.
② 八九成：指十分之八九。Eighty to ninety percent.
③ 趴：身体向前伏靠。Lean on, lie prone.
④ 瞪：睁大眼睛看。Stare, glower. ;
⑤ 今儿个：北方方言，今天。(Northern dialect) today.

朋友们笑着回答说:"不怪①天,不怪地,怪只怪你昨日不曾送客!"

13. You're to Blame for Not Seeing the Guests Off

One day Mr Pedant invited some friends home for a drink. During the course of drinking he fell asleep at the table.

When he awoke he thought he had slept for a whole night. He was astonished to see his friends still sitting around the table. Staring in amazement, he said, "I didn't send out any invitation cards for today. Why did you all come?" His friends laughed and replied:"You can blame neither Heaven nor earth. You yourself are to blame for not seeing off your guests!"

---

① 怪:抱怨,责备。Blame, complain.

14. 先洗衣服

有一天,迂公借了别人的一件衣服穿着出门,正好赶上下大雨。

迂公走着走着,一不小心,滑了一跤。弄脏了借来的衣服,而且还把胳膊摔断了。

陪着他的人一见,连忙把他扶起来,打算背他去找医生。迂公连忙阻止说:"你快些弄点水,先把这件衣服洗一洗,至于我的胳膊,你们不用管!"

陪着他的那个人说:"你已经摔成这个样子,为什么还去惦记①那一件衣服?"

迂公回答说:"嗨!你怎么这么不懂事!胳膊是我自己的,比不得这件衣服,不会有人来向我讨还的!"

---

① 惦记:心里老想着某件事或某个人,放心不下。Keep think-ing or worrying about.

14. Wash the Coat First

One day Mr Pedant went out in a coat he had borrowed from somebody. Unfortunately he was caught in a shower of rain.

While he was walking along he slipped and fell in a puddle. He broke his arm, and the coat got dirty.

A passer-by hastened to help him up and take him to a doctor. But Mr Pedant stopped him at once, crying "Wash the coat first. Don't bother about my arm!" Surprised, the man said, "You are hurt! Why are you worried about the coat?" Mr Pedant replied: "How can you be so thoughtless? The arm is mine, not like the coat. So nobody will come to ask for it back."

15. 宋笺①该由宋人题诗

迁公家里珍藏②着祖传的几幅宋笺，一直没舍得请人在上面题诗或作画。

有一天，从苏州来了一位擅长书法和绘画的名士③。有人见这是一个千载难逢④的好机会，便诚心诚意地奉劝⑤他说："您家里收藏的那几幅宋笺，精美无比⑥，为什么还不赶快拿出来，请这位苏州名士给题几首诗、作几幅画呢？"

迁公听了，误以为人家在戏弄⑦自己，于是没好气⑧地说："你难道想让那个人弄坏我的宋笺吧？既然是宋笺，理所当然⑨地就应该由宋朝人在上面题诗、作画。"

---

① 宋笺：笺是指小幅而华贵的纸张，常用以题咏、作画，此笺由宋代传留下来的，故名宋笺。A kind of expensive paper produced in the Song Dynasty（960－1279）and only used for inscriptions and paintings.

② 珍藏：珍重地收藏。也指所藏的珍宝。Collect（art treasures）；collection.

③ 名士：指以诗文等著称的人。A person with a literary reputation.

④ 千载难逢：一千年也难碰到一次。形容机会非常难得。Very rare, appearing only once in a thousand years.

⑤ 奉劝：劝告。Advice.

⑥ 精美无比：精细美妙，无法比拟。So exquisite that it is beyond comparison.

⑦ 戏弄：玩弄，捉弄。Tease；make fun of.

⑧ 没(méi)好气：因心情不愉快而态度不好。Upset, inimically.

⑨ 理所当然：按道理就该如此。Of course.

15. Only a Song Poet
Can Use Song Paper

In Mr Pedant's home there were some blank pieces of writing paper of the Song Dynasty collected by his ancestors. He treasured them very much.

One day a famous calligrapher and painter came from Suzhou. Someone urged Mr Pedant to take advantage of this very rare chance: "Those pieces of Song paper are exquisite beyond comparison. Why don't you invite this celebrity from Suzhou to inscribe a poem or execute a painting on one of them ?"

Mr Pedant thought the man was making fun of him, and replied irately: "Do you want him to ruin my paper? Since this is Song paper, of course only a Song poet or painter can work on it. "

16. 迂公盼贼①

　　某天夜里，有个小偷窜②到迂公家去偷东西。正在这时迂公突然回到家里。小偷一见来了人，惊惶失措③，连自己刚从别处偷来的一件羊皮大衣也没来得及拿，就越④墙逃跑了。迂公白拣到一件羊皮大衣，心里非常高兴。

----

　　① 贼：偷窃东西的人。Thief.
　　② 窜：乱跑。Run around.
　　③ 惊惶失措：惊慌惶恐，不知所措。Thrown into a panic.
　　④ 越：跨过。Climb, step over.

打这以后，迂公心里便总想着再这样拣它几件。因此，每当他夜里从外面回来，总要先看看有没有小偷。一见家里没有任何动静，他就皱起眉头，抱怨说："今天夜里怎么又没有小偷来呢!"

16. Mr Pedant Looks Forward to Being Burgled

One night Mr Pedant returned home just in time to disturb a burglar. In a panic, the intruder jumped over a wall and escaped, leaving behind a sheepskin overcoat he had stolen from somewhere else. Mr Pedant was delighted to get a sheepskin overcoat for nothing.

From then on every time Mr Pedant came back home at night, he always looked forward to seeing a burglar. Whenever he saw that his home had not been disturbed, he would grumble in disappointment.

17. 罚吃猪肉

李载仁是唐王朝①的后裔②,为人迂腐③呆痴,平生怕吃猪肉。在他看来,吃猪肉简直比吃药还要难受。

有一天,他刚骑上马准备出门,忽然有两个仆人打起架来。他一见很生气,连忙吩咐随从到厨房里取来一大盘猪肉,喝令④两个打架的仆人当场吃掉。两个仆人高兴地大口大口地吃猪肉,李载仁在旁边怒气冲冲地说道:"姑念⑤初犯,这次就只罚你们吃些猪肉,以后如敢再犯,就一定在猪肉里加上些酥油⑥,看你们怕也不怕?"

---

① 唐王朝:即唐朝(618—907),由李渊、李世民父子所建,历二十帝,二百九十年,为后梁朱温所灭。The Tang Dynasty (618—907) founded by Li Yuan and his son Li Shimin. There were 20 emperors during the 290 years of the dynasty, which was overthrown by Zhu Wen of the State of Late Liang.
② 后裔:后代,子孙。Descendant.
③ 迂腐:拘泥守旧。Stubbornly clinging to outworn rules and ideas.
④ 喝令:大声命令。Command loudly.
⑤ 姑念:姑,暂且。姑念意思是暂且看在……份上。姑,for the moment. Considering ... for the moment.
⑥ 酥油:牛羊乳制成的食品。Butter.

17. Eating Pork As a Punishment

Li Zairen was a descendant of the imperial
family of the Tang Dynasty. He was both bookish
and foolish, and particularly loathed pork. It
seemed to him that pork was more unbearable than
medicine.

One day, just after he had mounted his horse
ready to go out, he saw two of his servants fight-

ing. He was very angry and ordered his attendant to bring a big plate of pork from the kitchen and make the two servants eat it on the spot. The two men ate it with much delight and relish, but Li Zairen berated them thus: "I only made you eat pork this time, since it's the first time you have fought. But if you dare to do so again, I'll add some butter to the pork. And that will teach you a lesson, I'll bet!"

18. 迁公医狗眼

有一年夏天,迁公得了红眼病①,一连十多天也没见好转,只得去找医生治疗。

临出门时,迁公家里养的那条狗正好卧在台阶下。迁公本打算从狗身上跨过去,可一不小心,误踩在了狗脖子上。狗猛然受惊,起身就咬,把迁公的裤子撕了一道大口子。

迁公一五一十②地把这件事对医生说了一遍。这个医生和迁公是老熟人,便故意跟他开玩笑说:"这一定是您家的狗也害了眼病,不然的话,它又怎么会咬破您的衣裳呢?"

迁公在回家的路上,边走边想:狗害了眼病,咬主人事小,夜里被盗事大。于是,回到家里把药煎好以后,先让狗喝了个够。

---

① 红眼病:指一种因发炎而充血发红的眼病。Inflammation of the eyes.
② 一五一十:指叙述事情时从头到尾,清楚而无遗漏。(Tell) one by one.

18. Mr Pedant Treats a Dog's Eye Problem

One summer Mr Pedant was suffering from inflammation of the eyes. So he decided to consult a doctor.

When he was going out, his dog was lying on the doorstep. Mr Pedant intended to stride over the dog, but incidentally trod on its neck. The startled dog jumped up and tore at Mr Pedant's clothes.

When Mr Pedant recounted this tale to the doctor, an old friend of his, the doctor joked: "Your dog must have irritated eyes too. That's why it was so savage. " On his way back home, Mr Pedant thought, "It's a small matter for a dog to bite its master, but a big problem if a burglar breaks in at night. " Therefore, he concocted the medicinal herbs right after he got home and let the dog drink the lot.

19. 头发换糖

有个人见别人用头发能换糖,便误认为凡是吃的东西都可以用头发换。

有一天,他清早出门,往怀里揣了一把头发就上了路。走着走着,他见路旁有一家酒店,便进去饱饱地吃了一顿。吃完之后,当他用怀里的头发抵账时,店小二①们无不哈哈大笑。他见别人都在笑话他,便怒气冲冲②地说:"别人都能拿头发当钱用,为啥③轮到我就偏偏不行呢?"

店小二与他争吵了好久,见他身上确实未带分文④,便揪⑤住他的头发,把他乱捶⑥了一顿,然后将他赶出了门。

这人一边用手慢慢地梳理着自己的头发,一边冲⑦着店小二大喊大叫:"整把头发给你们,你们不要,反倒在我头上乱抢,真是岂有此理!"

---

① 店小二:旅店、酒楼、饭馆中招待顾客的人。Waiter.
② 怒气冲冲:形容非常生气。Very angrily.
③ 啥:什么。What?
④ 分文:指很少的钱。Penny.
⑤ 揪:抓住。Grab.
⑥ 捶:用拳头敲打。Beat with the fists.
⑦ 冲(chòng):朝着,向着。Toward.

19. Trading Hair for Sugar

A man saw someone selling hair in return for sugar, so he thought that anything edible could be bought with hair.

One morning he left home carrying in his pocket a hank of hair. On his way he saw a restaurant, walked in and ordered a big meal. When he finished, he offered the hank of hair to pay the bill. The waiters all burst out laughing. The man said indignantly: "If other people can use hair as money, why can't I?"

The waiters argued with him for a long while, then, as he was obviously penniless, they dragged him out of the restaurant by the hair.

The man shouted to the waiters while arranging his hair slowly with his fingers: "I offered you a whole hank of hair, and you didn't want it. So why did you try to steal the hair from my head?"

20. 只要一匹

从前有个商人，打算到苏州去买货。临行前，有人对他说："苏州人卖东西，总是多要一倍价钱，因此在买的时候，看他所要的价钱，只答应给他一半就行了。"这个商人信以为真①。

有一天，他来到一家绸缎店买绸缎，凡是店主开的价②，他一律杀价③一半。店主对他这样还价④很恼火⑤，于是没有好气地对他说："如果照你这样还价，你就不用买了。敝店⑥干脆送你两匹算了！"

这个商人连连作揖说："不敢！不敢！本人只要一匹就行了！"

---

① 信以为真：相信这是真的。Believe something to be true.
② 开价：交易中说出价格。Offer a price.
③ 杀价：压低价格。Demand a lower price.
④ 还价：买东西时说出愿付的价格。Counter-offer.
⑤ 恼火：生气，不愉快。Annoyed，irritated.
⑥ 敝店：谦称自己的商店。"My humble shop."

20. Only One Bolt Will Do

A merchant planned to make some purchases in Suzhou. Before he left, someone told him: "Suzhou people always charge double the price. So only offer half what they ask for." The merchant kept that in mind.

One day he went to a silk store to buy some silk and satin. He haggled over whatever price the shop-keeper offered and was adamant about paying only half. The shop-keeper said in a fit of pique: "Your bargaining is driving me crazy. If I give you two bolts of silk will you go away and leave me alone?"

The merchant bowed obsequiously and replied: "Oh no, only one bolt will do."

21. 原物未动

有个理发匠给一个和尚剃头时，一不留心①，把和尚的耳朵剃掉了一个，痛得和尚直②叫唤。

这时，理发匠不慌不忙③地从地上拣起耳朵，安慰和尚说："师父④不必着急，原物丝毫未动，全在我这儿呢！"

---

① 留心：留意，当心。Careful，take care.
② 直：不断地。Continuously.
③ 不慌不忙：形容说话、行动从容不迫。(Speak or act) calmly and unhurriedly.
④ 师父：对和尚、尼姑、道士的尊称。A respectful form of address for a monk or nun.

21. It's Totally Unhurt

A barber was shaving a monk's head. Unfortunately he cut off one of his customer's ears.

As the monk yelled in pain, the barber calmly picked up the ear and comforted him: "Please don't worry sir. It's totally unhurt. You see, it's all here in my hand."

22. 一概明天

有个负债的人,因事要出门,他怕债主认出自己向自己讨债,于是找来一项斗笠①戴在头上,这才匆匆上路。

刚出门没多远,就被一个债主认了出来,这个债主用手指弹着他的斗笠问道:"你答应还我的钱,准备得怎么样了?"负债人为了脱身,便随口应付②说:"明天。"

过了一会,突然下起冰雹,无数的雹子把负债人的斗笠砸得劈劈啪啪乱响。这人误以为又是要债的人在敲他的斗笠,吓得心慌意乱,连连答应:"明天!明天!一概明天!"

22. Tomorrow, Tomorrow

A man heavily in debt ventured out. Afraid of being recognized by his creditors, he put on a large bamboo hat.

---

① 斗笠:用竹篾、竹叶等编制成的宽边帽子,既可遮阳,又能挡雨。A broad-brimmed bamboo hat used for both shade from the sun and shelter from the rain.
② 应付:敷衍。Do something perfunctorily; stall somebody.

Shortly after he left home, he was spotted by a creditor, who tapped the hat, saying, "Are you ready to pay back the money you owe me?" He stalled the creditor with the answer: "Tomorrow."

Before long, it suddenly began to hail. The hailstones kept crackling and sputtering upon the debtor's hat. He thought a crowd of his creditors were tapping his hat again. So, in a panic, he repeatedly said: "Tomorrow, tomorrow."

23. 你怎么知道的？

两位苏州人在路上碰见了，一个人问另一个人："尊姓①?""姓张。"又问"尊号②?""东桥。"又问："贵府③何处?""阊门④外。"

---

① 尊姓：称呼对方的敬辞，就是姓什么的意思。A respectful way of asking somebody's surname.

② 号：名称，这里是指名字。Assumed name — here it means name.

③ 贵府：敬辞，意思为你的家。A respectful way of asking someone's address.

④ 阊门：城门名，指原先的苏州城西门。The former West City Gate of Suzhou.

问的人点点头说:"哦,您原来是阊门外的张东桥先生!"张东桥惊愕地说:"您怎么知道的呢?"问者说:"这些都是刚才您自己说的呀!"

23. How Did You Know?

Two men in Suzhou City met each other on the road. One man asked the other politely:"May I know your surname, please?" "My surname is Zhang." "Your given name please?" "Dongqiao." The man asked again:"And where is your home, please?" "Outside Lümen."

The first man then nodded his head and said: "Oh, I see. You are Mr Zhang Dongqiao from outside Lümen." Zhang Dongqiao was stunned:"How did you know that?" The man said:"That's what you just told me!"

24. 呆子拒盗

　　一个呆子听说强盗进了家门,急忙写了"各有内外"①四个字,贴在堂②前;听说强盗已经到了堂前,又急忙写了"此路不通"四个字,贴在内屋③前;听说强盗进了内屋,慌忙跑入厕所,强盗也跟着追到了厕所,他连忙掩④上厕所的门,大声咳嗽,说:"有人在此!"

---

　　① 各有内外:内外有别,意欲阻止强盗进入正房。"The inside is not the outside," a warning to burglars.
　　② 堂:指的是正房。The central room.
　　③ 内屋:即内室,这里指的是卧室。The bedroom.
　　④ 掩:关闭,合拢。Close (the door, window).

24. A Blockhead Tries to Stop a Burglar

A blockhead heard a burglar breaking into his house. He hurriedly wrote a note: "The inside is not the outside" and put it up on the door of the central room. When he heard the burglar reach the central room he hastened to write "Dead end" on a piece of paper and stuck it onto the door of the bedroom. After the burglar broke into the bedroom he rushed to the toilet. Closing the door in a flurry, he coughed loudly when he heard the burglar approach and shouted, "There's already somebody in!"

25. 情愿做儿子

一老头儿形容枯槁①，衰老不堪②，可最讨厌别人说他衰老；有人夸他少嫩，他就欢喜异常。

有一人知道他这种心意，假装讨他喜欢："您虽

---

① 形容枯槁：形体容貌憔悴枯萎。Sallow and withered appearance.

② 衰老不堪：年老而精力、体质非常衰弱。Very feeble and senile.

然须发①都白了,可容颜娇嫩,不单能同幼童相比,竟然与我刚生不久的儿子的皮肤一样。"老头听了,高兴地说:"我的容颜能够那么少嫩,老夫情愿做你的儿子。"

25. "I'd Rather Be Your Son"

An old man who looked haggard and decrepit hated most of all to be thought aged. If somebody praised him as looking young, it delighted him.

Knowing this, someone once pretended to flatter him:"Although your hair has turned white, you look so young and delicate that you can compare not only with young children but even with my new-born son." Upon hearing this, the old man was filled with joy:"If only I could look that tender, I'd rather be your son," he said.

① 须发:胡须和头发,这里泛指毛发。Hair and beard.

26. 擦干净刀口

一个人犯了死罪，绑至法场①，临开刀问斩②时，他对刽子手③说："求你把刀口擦干净！我听说杀头用的刀，如果刀口不干净，杀了头脖子上会生疮。现在你如果不把刀口擦干净，真的让我害起疮来，到什么时候才能好？"

---

① 法场：旧时执行死刑的场所。An old term for the execution ground.
② 开刀问斩：指执行斩刑。Decapitation.
③ 刽子手：旧时执行死刑的人。The executioner or headsman in olden times.

26. Clean the Blade

A criminal sentenced to death was sent to the execution ground. Right before the execution he said to the headsman: "Would you please clean the blade? I heard that when the edge of the sword is dirty, a carbuncle grows on the neck of a person beheaded. If you don't clean the blade and I get a carbuncle, how can I be cured?"

27. 存放在肚子里的牛奶

从前有个愚人①,准备宴请宾客。他打算存点牛奶,到时候让客人喝。他想:要是从现在开始每天挤奶,牛奶就会越来越多,最后连放牛奶的地方也没有,还有可能腐败变酸,倒不如干脆让它存放在牛肚子里,到请客那一天一下子把它们挤出来。

---

① 愚人:愚昧无知之人。A foolish and ignorant person.

想到这里,他连忙跑到牛圈,把母牛和小牛分开
拴。一个月以后,他准备好宴席招待客人,这才把母
牛牵来,准备挤奶,可是挤了半晌①,连一滴奶也没
有挤出来。

客人们见了,无不掩口而笑。

27. Storing Milk

Once a foolish man wanted to invite guests to a banquet the following month. Planning to prepare some milk for the guests to drink, he figured that if he milked his cow every day, there would be no place to store all the milk, and besides it might get sour. Better to keep it inside the cow, he thought, and when the day of the party comes, get it all at the same time.

With this in mind, he hurried to the cowshed and separated the cow from its calf. A month later, with the banquet ready for the guests, he brought the cow in and tried to milk it. But not a drop of milk came out.

Seeing this, his guests all burst into laughter.

---

① 半晌:方言。半天,好大一会儿。(Northern dialect) for a long time, quite a while.

28. 先盖第三层楼

从前有个财主，一次到一个富翁家，见人家有一座三层楼房，既高大壮丽，又宽敞明亮，心里顿①生羡慕。他想："我的钱财并不比他少，为什么就没有想到盖这样一座楼房呢？"

回到家里，他连忙找来木匠，问道："你会盖②三层楼房吗？"

木匠回答说："那个富翁的三层楼房就是我盖的。"

财主听了，高兴地说："现在你就给我盖一座同样的楼房。"

于是，木匠按照财主的吩咐，开始测量、挖沟、奠基。财主见了，疑惑不解地问木匠："你这是干什么？"

"给您盖三层楼房啊！"木匠回答说。

财主又说："我不想要下面两层，你可以先给我盖第三层。"

木匠回答说："世上哪有这样的事，不盖第一层怎么盖第二层？不盖第二层又怎么盖第三层呢？"

"我现在就是不要下两层，你一定要先给我盖第三层！"

---

① 顿：立刻，即时。At once, instantly.
② 盖：建筑。Build.

木匠听了，哭笑不得，只好住手停工。

28. "Build the Third Floor First"

Once a rich man went to another rich man's home. Seeing the three-story building was so spacious and majestic, he felt envious and thought, "I have as much money as he has. Why did I never think of building such a mansion?"

When he got home, he called a carpenter at once and asked him: "Can you build a three-story house?"

The carpenter replied, "Yes, I built that other rich man's three-story house."

The rich man was pleased and said, "Then build a similar house for me."

So the carpenter began to measure, dig and lay the foundations. But the rich man was puzzled and asked him: "Why are you doing this?"

"It's for your three-story house!" The carpenter answered.

"I don't want the first two floors. Build the third floor first."

"How on earth can I do that? Without the first floor, how can I build the second? Without the second, how can I build the third?"

"I simply don't want the first two. You must build the third floor for me first."

The carpenter didn't know whether to laugh or to cry. He could do nothing but just to pack up his tools and go home.

29. 种煮胡麻子①

从前有个蠢人,生吃胡麻子,觉得又苦又涩;煮熟了吃,又香又面②。于是他在心里琢磨③:"要是把煮熟的胡麻子种到地里,结出的胡麻子一定会很好吃。"后来,他煮了一锅胡麻子种到地里,结果一棵也没有长出来。

---

① 胡麻子:产于我国西北、内蒙古一带的油用亚麻的子,可以煮吃。Linseed or the seed of flax, edible after boiling, produced in Northwest China and Inner Mongolia.

② 面:北方方言。指某些食物纤维少而柔软。(Northern dialect) soft and floury.

③ 琢磨:思考,研究。Think over, ponder.

29. Planting Boiled Linseeds

Once there was a man who ate linseed raw and found it both bitter and astringent. But after he boiled it, it became savory and floury. He thought, "If I plant boiled linseed, what comes up will be very delicious. " So he boiled a whole pot of linseed and planted it. But not a single shoot came up.

30. 起死回生①

从前有个鲁国②人,名叫公孙绰,他经常对别人夸口说:"我能使人起死回生。"

---

① 起死回生:把快要死的人救活,形容医术高明。Referring to the superb skill of a doctor who can bring the dying back to life.

② 鲁国:古国名。The State of Lu in ancient China.

别人不相信,问他有什么办法。他回答说:"我治好过许多半身不遂①的病人,现在我把治半身不遂的药,加大一倍的剂量,不就可以使人起死回生了吗?"

30. Bringing the Dying Back to Life

Long ago there was a doctor in the State of Lu called Gongsun Chuo. He often bragged to people: "I can bring the dying back to life."

People didn't believe him and asked him how he could do it. He said, "I have cured many patients who suffered from hemiplegia. Now if I double the dosage of medicine for hemiplegia, shouldn't I be able to bring the dying back to life?"

---

① 半身不遂:即偏瘫。Hemiplegia.

31. 为什么偏偏姓万

　　河南有个土财主,家财万贯①,但祖祖辈辈没有一个人识字。

　　有一年,这个财主从外地请了一个教书先生,来教自己的儿子读书识字。第一天,先生教他握笔临帖②,写一画,告诉他说:"这是个'一'字。"写两画,告诉他:"这是个'二'字。"写三画,告诉他说:"这是个'三'字。"③教到这儿,那孩子把笔一扔,高高兴兴地对自己的父亲说:"孩儿全会了,孩儿全会了!不用再麻烦先生了,请您把先生辞了吧!"

　　土财主一听很高兴,于是拿出一些银子,辞退了教书先生。

　　过了些日子,土财主打算请一位姓万的朋友来喝酒,一早起来,就让儿子去写请帖。儿子写了大半晌,也没有写完。土财主心里很着急,便去催他快点写。这时,儿子气愤愤地说:"天下的姓这么多,为啥

---

　　① 家财万贯:形容家庭财产非常多。A very wealthy family.
　　② 临帖:照着字帖写字,学习书法的一种方法。Practicing calligraphy after a model.
　　③ 一,二,三:是 1,2,3 的中文字。土财主的儿子因此产生误会,认为"万"字就是一万画。一,二,三 are the Chinese characters for one, two and three. The rich man's son thought that 万 (ten thousand) should have 10,000 strokes.

他偏偏姓'万'，我从早上写到现在，还刚刚写完五百画。"

31. Why Should He Be Surnamed Wan?

A man in Henan was very wealthy, but he

came from an illiterate family.

He invited a teacher from out of town to teach his son how to read and write. On the first day, the teacher taught the boy how to hold a writing brush and copy a model of calligraphy. He wrote a horizontal stroke and told his pupil: "This is 'one'. " Then he wrote two strokes and said: "This is 'two'". After he wrote three strokes and told the boy it was "three", the boy threw the brush away and told his father: "I've learnt everything. We don't have to bother the teacher any more. Please let him go. "

The rich man was very happy to hear this. So he paid the teacher his salary and dismissed him.

Later, the rich man planned to invite a friend named Wan for a drink. After he got up in the morning he asked his son to write an invitation card. After writing for almost half the day, the son still had not finished it. The rich man got impatient and urged him to hurry up. Then the son said indignantly: "Of all the surnames in the world, why should he have the surname Wan? I've been writing hard from morning till now and have only just finished 500 strokes!"

32."言简意明"

有个人写起信来,词语重复,啰里啰唆①。有位朋友劝他说:"老兄②您的文笔③还可以,只是那些繁言絮语④应该去掉。以后再写信,只要言简意明就行了。"这个人听完,频频点头表示接受。

时隔不久,他又在给这位朋友的信中写道:"上次承蒙⑤您的高明指教,深为感激和敬佩,从此以后,我万不敢再用那烦琐冗长⑥的文字去打搅您的视听⑦了。"他又在"万"字的旁边加了如下一条小注⑧:"这个'万'字是'方'字上边没有那一点的'万'字,也就是那简写的'万'字。我本来打算恭恭敬敬地写那个草字头的繁写的'萬'字,只因匆匆忙忙,所以没来得及写那个草字头的繁写的'萬'字。总而言之,这封信写得很潦草,很不工整⑨,有失敬意,这还请

---

① 啰里啰唆:方言。指语言繁杂重复。Wordy.
② 老兄:男性朋友、熟人之间的尊称。A respectful form of address between male friends and acquaintances.
③ 文笔:指写作的技巧。Skill or style of writing.
④ 絮语:指絮絮叨叨的话。Long-winded words.
⑤ 承蒙:套语。受到。(Polite) be indebted to someone for a kindness.
⑥ 冗长:指文章、讲话又啰唆又长。Tediously long.
⑦ 视听:指视力和听力。Seeing and hearing.
⑧ 注:用来解释的文字。Note.
⑨ 工整:精细整齐。Neat.

您多加原谅，多加包涵^①！"

32. Terse and Concise

A certain man was very verbose and liked to
repeat himself in his letters. A friend of his ad-
vised him："Your writing is fine, only you should

---

① 包涵：套语。请人原谅。Excuse, forgive.

get rid of all those redundant parts. Just be concise and terse when you write letters. " The man nodded in agreement.

Before long, he wrote another letter to this friend: "I'm very grateful for the brilliant advice you gave me last time, which I accept with great respect. From now on I absolutely dare not disturb your eyes with my over-elaborate and tediously long writing. " Then he added a note beside the character 万: "This is a simplified 万, i. e. , a 方 without the dot. I meant to write the unsimplified 萬 with the grass radical on top respectfully. But as I was in such a hurry I didn't have the time to write 萬 with the grass radical on top. In short, this letter is written so hastily and carelessly that it might seem disrespectful. Please forgive me for this poorly written and messy letter. "

33. 是哪个月上走的？

作揖①是我国古代的一种礼节。朋友熟人相见，总要先作上一个揖，以表示对对方的尊敬。

有个年轻人平时作揖，因为太快，好像有点不礼貌，所以得罪了不少人。有位长辈教他说："你往后再作揖时，一边作一边默念正月②、二月、三月、四月……一直默念到十二月，才把揖作完，这样就会自然而然③地慢下来。"他听了连连点头。

第二天，这个年轻人出门时，正好在路上遇到一个朋友，他便按照那个长辈教他的那样，给这个朋友作起揖来。他一边作揖，一边"正月、二月……"往下念，而且念得特别慢。等到他作完揖，那个朋友已经走远了。于是，他问站在旁边的人说："我这朋友是哪个月上走的？"

---

① 作揖：两手抱拳高拱，身体略弯，向人行礼。Make a bow (by clasping one's hands in front of one's chest).

② 正月：农历一年的第一个月，即一月。The first month according to the lunar calendar.

③ 自然而然：自然，不受外力影响，自由发展。然，如此这样。自然，naturally. 然，like this.

33. In Which Month Did He Leave?

Making a bow with the hands clasped in front of the chest was an ancient form of Chinese etiquette. When friends and acquaintances met they always made such bows to show respect for each other.

There was a young man who released his

hands too quickly when making bows, thereby offending many people who interpreted this as impolite. An elderly person told him: "When you make bows, just recite silently January, February, March ... and keep your hands clasped until you reach December. In this way, you'll certainly slow down." The young man nodded his head and accepted his advice.

The next day, when the young man went out he happened to meet a friend. He made a bow while reciting silently January, February, etc., making a point of reciting slowly. When he finished, his friend was already out of sight. He thereupon asked a bystander: "In what month did my friend leave?"

34. 上任①问例②

从前有个新官刚到任,就问自己的下属说:"官应该怎么当才好?"

下属说:"头一年③要清④,先落个好名声;第二年要半清半混,不能太过分;第三年就可以为所欲为⑤了。"

新官听后,连声长叹:"叫我怎么才能熬⑥到第三年,叫我怎么才能熬到第三年啊!"

34. A New Official Asks About the Rules

An official who had just taken up a post asked his subordinate:"How should an official behave?"

His subordinate said, "In the first year just be honest and earn a good reputation. In the second year you can be half dishonest but do not go too far. In the third year you can do whatever you

---

① 上任:指官员就职。Take up an official post.
② 例:规律、规则、常规。Rules, routine.
③ 头一年:第一年。The first year.
④ 清:廉洁。Honest.
⑤ 为所欲为:想怎么干就怎么干。Do whatever one likes.
⑥ 熬:忍受,挨过。Suffer, endure.

please."

The official signed repeatedly: "How can I hold out till the third year? How can I endure the first two years?"

35. 有钱者生

从前,有个管菜园的老头儿种茄子 怎么也种不活,他常常为这件事而苦恼. 被迫无奈①,他只好去向一个老菜农请教种茄子的方法。

老菜农告诉他:"你在每棵茄子旁边,埋上一枚铜钱②,保管会活。"

管菜园的老头儿一听,觉得很奇怪,便问是什么缘故③。老菜农对他说:"你难道没有听说过,如今的世道④是'有钱者生,无钱者死'吗?"

35. Those With Money Survive

There was a gardener who just couldn't get egg-plants to grow. Vexed with this for a long time, he turned to an old vegetable grower for advice.

The old vegetable grower told him: "Bury a coin beside each egg-plant. I'm sure they will sur-

---

① 无奈:无可奈何。Have no way out.
② 铜钱:铜铸的钱币。Copper coin.
③ 缘故:原故,原因。Reason.
④ 世道:社会状况,风气。Common social practice and morals of the time.

vive. "

The gardener was puzzled and asked the reason. The old vegetable grower said: "Haven't you heard that nowadays those with money survive and those without it die?"

36. 古物

南朝①宋的江夏②王刘义恭,嗜好搜集古物,经常向在朝公卿索要。侍中③何勖已经送过了,可是刘义恭还是一个劲地索求,何勖心里很是不满。

这一天,何勖走在道上,见路旁扔着一副狗脖子上戴的铁环和一条破犊鼻裈④,便命随从⑤拣回家,装进箱子,送给刘义恭,并附信道:"现送上秦相⑥李斯⑦打猎时所牵黄狗戴的铁环一具,汉⑧司马相如⑨卖酒时所穿的犊鼻裈一条。"

---

① 南朝:朝代名,从 420 年刘裕代晋到 589 年陈亡,经历宋、齐、梁、陈四代。The Southern Dynasties（420－589）：Song, Qi, Liang, Chen.

② 江夏:古地名,在今湖北省。Name of a place in today's Hubei Province.

③ 侍中:旧官名,职位相当宰相。An ancient official title, equivalent to prime minister.

④ 犊鼻裈:短裤,围裙。Shorts and apron.

⑤ 随从:跟随官员的人员。Attendants.

⑥ 秦(公元前 221－公元前 206 年)相:秦朝宰相。A prime minister of the Qin Dynasty（221 BC－AD 206）.

⑦ 李斯(前? －前 208 年):秦朝宰相,政治家。Li Si（? －208 BC）, a politician and once prime minister of the Qin Dynasty.

⑧ 汉:朝代名,刘邦灭秦后于公元前 202 年建立,至公元 220 年曹丕称帝灭亡。The Han Dynasty（202BC-AD220）, founded by Emperor Liu Bang, fell to its doom in 220 when Cao Pi proclaimed to be the emperor of the State of Wei.

⑨ 司马相如(前 179 年－前 117 年):西汉辞赋家。相传司马相如与卓文君相恋私奔,因家贫,无以为生,当垆卖酒。二人故事,遂成佳话。Sima Xiangru（179 BC－117 BC）, a poet and prose writer of the Western Han Dynasty. A story goes that he and Zhuo Wenjun were deeply in love and had an elopement. As they were so poor, they had to open a wine shop to make a living.

36. The Relic Collector

Liu Yigong, the Duke of Jiangxia in the early part of Southern Dynasties, was especially fond of collecting relics. He was always asking his ministers and officials to give him such treasures. Prime Minister He Xu had already presented him with a gift, but he still pestered him for more. He Xu was very unhappy about this.

One day when He Xu was taking a walk he saw by the roadside an iron dog collar and a worn-out apron. He ordered his servant to take them home and send them to Liu Yigong in a box together with a letter: "Presented here are an iron ring that Qin Prime Minister Li Si's dog wore when he took it out hunting and an apron that Sima Xiangru of the Han Dynasty wore when he was selling wine."

37. 张鸬鹚①

神泉县令张某,表面廉洁,实际上是个贪得无厌②的人。

一天,他把一张布告悬挂在城门上:"某月某日,是本县③的生日,请大家不要送礼,特此告知。"

有个小吏看后对大家说:"县太爷说不让送礼,那是自谦,我们还得送。"到县令生日那一天,每个人都送上了礼物——绢绸,县令一一④收了。

过了不久,县令又贴出一张布告:"后月某日,是县君⑤生日,更不要送礼。"

大家一看,没有不耻笑⑥的。有人做了《鸬鹚》诗讽刺说:"飞来疑是鹤,下处却寻鱼⑦。"

---

① 鸬鹚:亦称"鱼鹰"。栖息河川、湖沼、海滨,善潜水捕食鱼类。Cormorant.
② 贪得无厌:贪心没有满足的时候。Have insatiable greed and desires.
③ 本县:县令的自称。The way a governor refers to himself.
④ 一一:一个一个地。One by one.
⑤ 县君:县令的妻子。The wife of a county governor.
⑥ 耻笑:鄙视嘲笑。Deride, ridicule, mock.
⑦ "飞来疑是鹤,下处却寻鱼":飞时好像是白鹤,停下来一看,却是一只找鱼吃的鸬鹚。讽刺县令表面廉洁实际上贪得无厌。An analogy between the governor and a bird which looks like a crane but is actually a fish-eating cormorant. A satire on the greedy, hypocritical governor.

37. Cormorant Zhang

Mr Zhang, the county governor of Shenquan, whose greed was insatiable, still managed to appear to keep his hands clean.

One day, he put up a poster on the city gate which read: "A certain day of a certain month is the governor's birthday. It is hereby announced that nobody should send any gifts."

A petty official said to his fellow officials after reading this: "The governor is very self-effacing to ask us not to send him any gifts. But still we must present him with something." So on the birthday of the governor everybody gave him a gift of precious silk, and the governor, of course, accepted all of them.

Before long, the governor put up another poster: "A certain day of the month after next is the governor's wife's birthday. You are expected not to send any gifts."

Everybody derided the governor after reading this poster. Someone ridiculed him by writing a poem titled *The Cormorant*: "A bird flying over, looking like a crane but stopping for fish, turned out to be a cormorant."

38. 暂且放到靴①筒里

有个县官因贪脏枉法②锒铛③入狱,好容易④熬到朝廷大赦⑤才得以免刑。因此,他发誓赌咒⑥:"从今以后,决不再接受别人的钱财,否则,就让我手上生恶疮⑦!"

复官不久,有个打官司的给他送来百两纹银⑧,求他从中帮忙把官司打赢。因为自己刚刚发过誓,赌过咒,他不敢再用手去接银子。停了一会,他忽然想出一个好办法,于是对那个送银子的说:"你既然如此恳切⑨,就请你暂且把银子放到我的靴筒里吧!"

---

① 靴:长筒鞋。中国古时为官的穿的鞋子。Boots worn by officials in ancient China.
② 贪脏枉法:贪污受贿,违法乱纪。Bribery and embezzlement.
③ 锒铛:铁锁链。这里指用铁锁链锁住。Shackles. Here: to be chained up.
④ 好容易:指做某件事非常不容易。With great difficulty.
⑤ 大赦:依法对犯人实行减刑或免刑。Amnesty.
⑥ 赌咒:即发誓。Swear, vow.
⑦ 恶疮:非常严重的皮肤溃烂病。Very serious skin ulcer.
⑧ 纹银:指成色最好的银子。Best quality silver.
⑨ 恳切:诚挚殷切。Earnestly, sincerely.

38. Just Put It in My Boots

A county official was thrown into prison for accepting bribes. After served years he was released by an amnesty. So he swore: "From now on, I shall not accept bribes. If I do, let my hands be covered with malignant boils."

After he was reinstated, a man pursuing a

lawsuit offered him 100 *liang* of the best quality silver, asking him for help in winning the lawsuit. The official dared not accept the silver with his hands. He paused for a while, and then said, "Since you're so sincere, please just put it in my boots."

39. 判棺材

一个姓张的和一个姓贾的,合着打到了一条大鱼。二人你争我夺,互不相让,各自都想独占,最后动手厮打起来。打了半晌,也没有打出结果,最后只好到官府了结①。

官老爷一见大鱼,心中暗喜。草草②问了几句,就马上判决说:"二人姓张姓贾,因为争鱼厮打,两人各去安生③,留下鱼儿让我老爷做鲊④。"说完,便命衙役把他俩赶出了衙门。

二人大失所望⑤,十分后悔,便合议去买一口棺材⑥假装争吵,再到官府去告状。心想官老爷也忌讳死人用的东西,决不会收留。

官老爷见二人抬着一口棺材来告状,又不假思索⑦地判决:"二人姓张姓贾,为争棺材厮打,棺盖给你们抬走,棺材底送给我老爷喂马。"说完,又命衙役把他俩赶出了衙门。

---

① 了结:解决,结束。Solve,bring to an end.
② 草草:草率,匆匆忙忙。Hastily,perfunctorily.
③ 安生:安定,安静。Calm down;be settled
④ 做鲊(zhǎ):加工制作腌鱼。Preserve a fish in salt.
⑤ 大失所望:非常失望。Very disappointed.
⑥ 棺材:用木料制成的装殓死人的器具。Coffin.
⑦ 不假思索:用不着考虑,形容办事说话反应迅速。Without thinking,readily,promptly.

39. Judgment on a Coffin

Mr Zhang and Mr Jia caught a big fish together. Each of them wanted the fish for himself, and
they argued for a long time. Finally they came to

blows. But after fighting for a long while they still could not get anywhere. So they had to resort to the local magistrate for judgment.

Seeing the big fish the magistrate was delighted. He asked some perfunctory questions and announced that as the disputants could not agree on the ownership of the fish, it should be forfeited to the magistrate himself. Then he ordered his constables to drive Mr Zhang and Mr Jia out.

The two were disappointed. They decided to buy a coffin and, pretending to wrangle over it, go to the local magistrate again. They figured that the magistrate would not keep it because it was for a dead person.

When the magistrate saw the two men coming again carrying a coffin, he made a ready judgment: "Mr Zhang and Mr Jia had a fight over a coffin. Now it is decided that they must take the lid away and leave the rest as a manger for the magistrate's horse." Then he ordered the constables to drive them out again.

40. 偷鞋刺史①

密州②刺史郑仁凯，既贪③又奸④。他的一个家奴鞋破得不能穿了，要求换双新的。郑仁凯便让一个穿着新鞋的小吏上树摘果子，令家奴趁机把鞋偷走。小吏从树上下来看见鞋子没有了，忙禀告⑤郑仁凯。郑仁凯回答道："我又不是给你看守鞋的刺史。"

① 刺史：旧官名。Prefectural governor, an old official title.
② 密州：旧地名，在今山东省。Ancient name of a place in present-day Shandong Province.
③ 贪：爱财。Greedy.
④ 奸：邪恶。Treacherous, crafty.
⑤ 禀告：把事情告诉上级。Report to one's superior.

40. Shoe-Stealing Governor

Zheng Renkai, the prefectural governor of Mizhou, was both greedy and crafty. One day a servant asked him for a pair of new shoes. Zheng Renkai ordered one of his subordinates who was wearing new shoes to climb a tree and pick some fruit. He then told his servant to steal the shoes, which had been left at the foot of the tree. When the other man got down from the tree and found his new shoes gone, he at once reported this to Zheng Renkai. But the later replied: "I'm the prefectural governor; I'm not responsible for guarding your shoes."

41. 试荆

幽州①总管②隋燕荣看见路旁长着的荆条③很宜做打人的鞭子,便用来在一个人身上试打。那个人说:"我没有罪,凭④什么打我?"

---

① 幽州:旧地名,在今河北、辽宁一带。An old name for a place in today's Hebei and Liaoning provinces.

② 总管:旧官名。An old official post.

③ 荆条:野生灌木的枝条,古时常做为刑杖。Twigs used to inflict punishment in ancient times.

④ 凭:依据。Base on; go by.

隋燕荣说:"先试打一下,以后有罪就免了。"

后来,那个人果然犯了错,隋燕荣要打他。他说:"您以前答应过我可以免罚的。"

隋燕荣说:"不犯错还可以打,何况①你今天犯了错呢?

随后又将那个人毒②打了一顿。

41. Trying Whips

Youzhou administrator Sui Yanrong saw that the twigs of the chaste trees growing along a road would make good whips, so he tried them out by whipping a man. The man said: "I'm not a criminal. Why do you whip me?"

Sui Yanrong said: "This is just a trial whipping. If you commit a crime in the future, you will be exempt from punishment."

Later, when the man did commit a crime, Sui Yanrong ordered him given a whipping. When the man argued, "You promised before that I would be exempt from punishment," Sui Yanrong said, "If

---

① 何况:用于反问,表示更进一层。Let alone, moreover; used in rhetorical questions.

② 毒:毒辣,酷烈。Cruelly, fiercely.

you could be whipped without committing any of-
fense before, today you can certainly be punished
when you have committed one. "

42. 我看老爷是糊涂的

从前有个睁眼瞎子①，平白无故②地被牵涉到一起偷盗案子里。

来到公堂③之上，这个睁眼瞎子说自己是个青光眼④，什么也看不见，因此与此案无关。

---

① 睁眼瞎子：即青光眼。Refers to glaucoma.
② 平白无故：指无缘无故。Without reason.
③ 公堂：旧指官署或法庭的庭堂。Old term for a law court.
④ 青光眼：眼内压力增高引起的眼病，重者视力消失。Glaucoma, that can cause blindness.

县官听后,把惊堂木①一拍,厉声喝道:"大胆刁民②,你的一双眼黑是黑、白是白,为何要撒谎说瞎?先给我打十五大板!"

这个睁眼瞎子看再争辩也无用,只好一语双关③地回答说:"老爷看小人是清白④的,可小人看老爷是糊涂的!"

42. You Are a Muddy Blur

Once a man suffering from glaucoma was involved in a larceny case.

When he was taken to court, he said that he was blind, so he had nothing to do with the case.

On hearing this, the county governor, who was sitting in judgment, banged the table with his gavel and shouted, "You bold, cunning man! Your eyes are obviously clear. Why do you say that you're blind? Give him 15 strokes!"

Seeing there was no use arguing with him, the

① 惊堂木:旧时官吏审案时拍案警戒受审者的小木块。Wooden gavel used by judges in the past.
② 刁民:刁钻的人,旧时官吏辱骂百姓的话。A curse used in the past by officials to insult common people.
③ 一语双关:一句话字面上一个意思,暗含着另一个意思。Pun.
④ 清白:纯洁,没有污点。Clean, innocent.

man replied with a pun: "In your eyes, sir, I'm as clear as crystal, but in my eyes, you are a muddy blur."

43. 本地神仙请不来

有个悭吝人,请道士来他家做法事①。道士请的神仙都是千里之外的,本地的神仙一位也没请。

这个悭吝人觉得很奇怪,便问道士说:"为啥都请这么远的?"

道士回答说:"近处的神仙都知道你从来不请客,说请他们,他们都不相信,也不会来!"

---

① 法事:指教徒诵经、讲法、修行、求仙等事。Religious services or rituals.

43. The Local Immortals Would Not Come

A stingy man invited a Daoist priest to hold a ceremony at his home. All the immortals the priest invited were from far-away places, and none was local.

The stingy man was surprised, and asked the priest: "Why did you only invite immortals from so far away?"

The priest replied: "The local immortals all know that you never invite people to your home. If I told them they were invited, they wouldn't believe it, and so no one would come."

44. 蘸着喝酒

从前有一户人家,父子俩都很吝啬,但非常好喝酒。在家里,他们每天都要喝酒。可是,每天的买酒钱从来没有超过一文①,因此买的酒也很少。为了防止一下子把酒喝完,父子俩相互约定,都只准用筷子头蘸着喝。

---

① 一文:文是旧时的小铜钱,一文就是一个小铜钱,表示很少的钱。Penny, copper coin.

有一天,两人喝酒时,儿子用筷子头连着蘸了两下。父亲看见后,一边用筷子猛敲儿子的头,一边大骂道:"你这个狗杂种,怎么吃酒吃得这样急!"

44. Drinking by Dips

Once there was a father and a son, both misers yet fond of wine. They drank at home every day but the drink never cost more than a penny. As the wine was so little, they had an agreement that each should only drink by dipping the tips of chopsticks into it, so that it should last longer.

One day when they were having a drink, the son dipped his chopsticks twice into the wine. Seeing this, the father rapped him on the head with his chopsticks and scolded him roundly: "You scoundrel! Are you trying to hog all the wine?"

45. 藕大如船

有个吝啬鬼用藕梢招待客人，把中间的大段大段的好藕留在厨房里，供自己以后食用。

有个客人看他待客这样小气，便故意对他说："我平时经常读诗，记得有两句是这样写的：'太华峰头玉井莲①，开花十丈②藕如船。'我一直怀疑没有这么长的藕，今天我才相信这两句诗写的并不错。"

---

① 太华峰头玉井莲：太华峰就是华山西峰，据说山顶有池，池里生有千叶莲花，亦称莲花峰。On Taihua Peak on Mount Hua there is a large lotus pond. Hence the peak is also called Lotus Peak.

② 丈：长度单位，十尺为一丈，折合为国际制 3.33 米。A Chinese unit of length, = 3.33 meters.

"为什么呢?"主人连忙问道。

这个客人用手指着桌子上的藕梢说:"你看这藕,藕梢已经到这里了,可那藕肚子还在厨房里!"

45. Lotus Root As Big As Boat

There was a miser who once entertained his guests with the ends of lotus roots, saving the better medium part in the kitchen for himself.

Seeing that he was such a mean host, a guest said to him:"I read poems quite often, and I remember two lines which go like this: 'In the lotus pond on Taihua Pick, the roots of the 30-feet-long lotus flowers are as big as boats.' I always doubted if there were any lotus roots as long as that. But today I believe the poet was right."

"Why?" The host asked.

Pointing to the ends of lotus root on the table, the guest said:"You see, the ends have reached here, but the main parts are still in the kitchen!"

46. 借灯

有个人请客时,只备了很少一点菜,客人们没吃几口就吃得一干二净。

这时候,有个客人对主人说:"请您借给我一盏灯。"

主人不解其意,问道:"大天白日,借灯干什么?"

客人说:"桌子上的菜,一点也看不见了,想借盏灯照一照。"

46. Borrowing a Lamp

A man invited some people to dinner but only provided a few dishes. The guests had only just started eating when the food was all gone.

One guest said to the host: "May I borrow a lamp please?"

The host was puzzled and asked: "What do you want to borrow a lamp for in broad daylight?"

The guest replied: "I can't see any food on the table, so I just want to use a lamp to have a better look!"

47. 锯酒杯

有个人被邀去赴宴,席间,主人斟酒,每次只斟半杯。他见主人这样吝啬,于是对主人说:"贵府如果有锯,请借给我用一下。"主人问他借锯干什么,他用手指着酒杯说:"这酒杯上半截既然不盛酒,就该锯去,留它空着有什么用?"

47. Sawing the Glass in Half

A man was invited to a banquet. Each time the host poured him some wine he only filled the glass half full. The man said to the stingy host: "If you have a saw, I would like to use it."

The host asked him what he wanted to use it for. The guest pointed at the glass and said, "Since the top half of the glass doesn't work, it should be cut off. Why leave it here holding nothing?"

48. 赏黄历^①

除夕,有个人给一个财主送年礼。这个财主收下之后,把一本老黄历赏给了送礼的。家里的仆人见了说:"这是本老黄历,赏给人家有什么用?"

这个财主瞪了仆人一眼,说:"不赏给他,我留着又有什么用!"

---

① 黄历:指历书。Almanac.

48. A Present of an Old Almanac

Someone presented a rich man with a gift on New Year's Eve. The rich man readily accepted it and then gave him an old almanac in return. His servant said, "This almanac is out of date, so what's the use of giving it to him?"

The rich man glowered at him and said, "What's the use of me keeping it?"

49. 别让旁人看见你的脸

　　古时候,有个十分悭吝的财主,想请一位画师为自己画一幅小像。但连纸墨酬金一共才给画师三分银子。这位画师也不讨价,挥起画笔在一张荆川纸①上给财主画了一幅背面像。

---

　　① 荆川纸:一种毛笔书画用纸。A special kind of paper for painting and calligraphy.

财主一见很奇怪,指着那幅背面像问画师:"画像神韵全在面部,你怎么给我画的是背面像呢?"

画师回答道:"你这么省银子,我劝你最好别让旁人看见你的脸!"

49. Don't Let People See Your Face

Long ago there was a very stingy rich man who invited a painter to paint his portrait. Altogether he gave the painter only one and a half grams of silver, including payment for paper and ink. Without bargaining, the painter drew a portrait of the rich man's back on a piece of Jingchuan paper.

The rich man felt puzzled. Pointing at the portrait of his back, he said to the painter: "The charm of a portrait is in the face. Why did you paint my back?"

The painter replied: "As you're so stingy, I think you'd better not let people see your face!"

50. 收拾骨头

一个书童每日辛辛苦苦伺候主人。可是每天吃饭,主人总是把菜肴吃的干干净净,只剩下一堆骨头在碗里。

书童很有怨气,便对天祷告道:"愿我们的相公①活一百岁,小人活一百零一岁。"

---

① 相公:仆人对男性主人的称呼。A term of address used by servants for their master.

主人很奇怪，问他为什么如此祷告。书童答道：
"小人多活一岁，好收拾相公的骨头呀！"

50. Collecting Bones

A servant worked very hard for his master every day. Yet at every meal the master always ate up all the food, leaving the servant only a few bones.

The servant was very resentful of this, so he prayed aloud one day: "May our master live to be one hundred, and I live to be one hundred and one."

Greatly puzzled, his master asked why he prayed like this. The servant answered: "I want to live one year more than you, so that I can collect your bones."

51. 冬冬汤

一个人平时又吝啬，又爱开玩笑。有一天，几个朋友闹①着要他请客，他便写了请柬与众人相约，"明天早晨，我要备下有音乐助兴的宴席，请诸位光临②一叙。"朋友们接了请柬，很是高兴。

第二天一大早，客人兴致勃勃地赶来。就坐③之后，主人仅端出两大盘冬瓜和一碗清汤，客人虽然很扫兴④，可是肚子实在饿了，也没多说，拿起筷子就吃起来，不一会儿，就吃得盘碗精光⑤。

这时主人又端出两盘冬瓜和一碗清汤。客人依旧又吃得精光，然后问道："老兄的盛宴我们是领教了，只是不知道您那助兴的音乐在哪儿。"

"诸位还没明白吗？"主人指着盘碗笑道，"冬冬汤，冬冬汤⑥！"

---

① 闹：吵，搅扰。Make a noise, trouble. Here：joke.
② 光临：敬称客人来到。(Of a guest) be present.
③ 就坐：在规定的座位上坐下。Sit down as arranged by the host.
④ 扫兴：遇到不愉快的事情而使兴致低落。Be disappointed.
⑤ 精光：一点儿不剩。With nothing left.
⑥ 冬冬汤：冬与咚、汤与喤同音。两盘冬瓜为咚咚，一碗清汤为喤，咚咚喤为鼓和锣敲出的声音，似音乐。冬, the first part of 冬瓜 (white gourd), is a homonym of 咚, the sound of a drum. 汤, sounds the same as 喤, the noise of a gong. Here the host thought that two plates of white gourd, Dong—Dong, and a bowl of soup, Tang, should sound like Dong—Dong Tang, an ensemble of the percussion instruments drum and gong.

51. Dong — Dong Tang

There was a miser who liked to play jokes. One day some friends made fun of him by pressing him to give a dinner. He then wrote them an invitation: "Tomorrow morning I will prepare a banquet accompanied by music. Your presence is cordially requested for the gathering. " His friends were very pleased.

Early the next morning, his guests arrived in high spirits. After everybody had taken his seat, the host only brought out two big plates of white gourd and a bowl of clear soup. Though disappointed, the hungry guests picked up their chopsticks and ate up all the white gourd and soup, without any comment.

Then the host served another two plates of white gourd and a bowl of clear soup. Again, the guests finished all of them. Then someone asked: "We've enjoyed your banquet. Now where is the music to accompany the meal?"

The host beamed and, pointed to the plates and bowl, said, "Dong—Dong Tang, Dong—Dong Tang. "

52. 我真的不识一字

有个财主请教书先生来教自己的儿子。先生刚一到，财主便道："我家没什么钱，恐怕要有不少失礼的地方，请多包涵。"

先生道："您何必如此客气，我本是个什么都可以将就①的人。"

"那好，"主人道，"我们是只吃青菜，不沾荤腥②，可以吗？"

"可以。"

"我家没有仆人，像那些打扫院落③、看守门户之类的事，要有劳④先生代管，可以吗？"

"可以。"

"有时家里的女人孩子们要买些零星⑤东西，也要委屈⑥先生跑跑腿⑦，可以吗？"

"可以。"

"果能如此，那真是太好啦！"

---

① 将就：迁就，勉强应付。Make do with, put up with.
② 荤腥：指鱼肉等食品。Meat and fish.
③ 院落：指庭院。Courtyard.
④ 有劳：用于拜托或答谢别人代自己做事的套语。Sorry to have caused you so much trouble.
⑤ 零星：零碎，零散。Odd, fragmentary.
⑥ 委屈：曲意迁就。Put up with, put somebody to great inconvenience.
⑦ 跑腿：为某种事务而奔走。Run an errand.

124

"但我也有一言相告,望主人不要感到吃惊。"先生道。

主人问先生要说什么。

先生道:"我只是惭愧自幼不曾读书。"

主人道:"先生何必如此谦逊!"

"实不相瞒,我真的不识一字。"

52. I Don't Know a Single Character

A miser invited a tutor to teach his son. As soon as the tutor arrived, the miser told him: "We are not rich. Please excuse us if there are things not quite up to your standards. "

The tutor said, "You are too polite. I'm the kind of person who can put up with anything. "

"Very well ," the host said. "We eat only vegetables, never any meat. Is that all right with you?"

"Yes. "

"Also we don't have a servant at home. So maybe we can trouble you to take care of things like sweeping the yard and opening the door for visitors?"

"Of course. "

"Sometimes my wife and children may want to buy something. May we bother you to run the errands?"

"Yes. "

"That's wonderful. "

The tutor then said, "But I also may not be up

to your standards as a tutor. "The host asked what he meant, and the tutor told him: "I am ashamed that I never learned to read. "

The host said: "You don't have to be so modest!"

"To tell you the truth, I don't even know one character. "

53. 一点也听不见

甲乙两个朋友,平时交往甚密,好得无话不谈。

有一天,甲突然卧病在床。乙听说以后,便赶忙去探望。他来到甲家,坐在甲的床边,握着甲的手对甲说:"老弟得的是什么病?你若需要什么东西,请尽管对我说,我一定千方百计给老弟办到!"

甲见乙这样诚心诚意,便对乙说:"不瞒老兄说,我是为二三钱银子愁病的。如果老兄您手头现成①,就请暂时借给我用一用,日后一定如数偿还!"

乙听甲这样说,马上装出一副没有听见的样子,吞吞吐吐②地对甲说:"老弟您说什么? 我怎么一点儿也听不见!"

53. Convenient Deafness

A and B were close friends who kept no secrets from each other.

One day A suddenly fell ill. Hearing of this, B

---

① 现成:眼前就有的,不必临时做或出力取得的。At hand, ready.

② 吞吞吐吐:形容说话迟疑或有话不敢说。Hesitate (in speech).

went to A's home at once. He sat by A's bed, held his hand and said: "What's wrong with you? If you need anything, just tell me. I'll do my best for you!"

As B was so sincere and earnest, A told him. "To tell you the truth, what made me sick was that I was worried about a few *liang* of silver. If you have some with you, please let me borrow it. I'll be sure to return it to you later."

When B heard this, he pretended that he hadn't heard. He hemmed and hawed, and said, "What did you say? How come I can't hear anything!"

54. 庸医①教子

有个庸医治死了人,被人家用绳子捆住,准备第二天送到官府惩治。夜里,庸医挣断绳子,趁着天黑,跳进河里游水而逃。

逃到家里,庸医看见儿子正在灯下攻读②医书,连忙对儿子说:"儿呀儿,你先别忙读这医书,还是先学会游泳要紧!"

---

① 庸医:医术低劣的医生。A quack doctor.
② 攻读:努力读书或钻研某种学问。Study hard.

54. A Quack Doctor Teaches His Son

A quack doctor ended up killing one of his patients. Therefore, the victim's family tied him up in order to take him to court the next day. At night the quack struggled free, jumped into a river and escaped in the darkness.

When he got home, he saw that his son was studying a medical book. He lost no time advising him: "My dear son, don't busy yourself with the medical book right now. It's more important to learn to swim first!"

55. 担心把肠子笑断

甲乙丙丁四个秀才都爱做诗,于是结为诗友①。

一天,四人一块到郊外去春游,看到河对面有座塔,不由②诗兴大发,吟③起诗来。

甲:"远望一座塔,"

乙:"近看也是塔;"

丙:"越看越像塔,"

丁:"原来就是塔。"

四个吟罢,互相称赞一番。这时,甲忽然对三个诗友说:"古人云④:'天资聪颖,必损寿命。'我等四人出口成章⑤,说明我们是绝顶⑥的聪颖。这样看来,我们四人定要短命夭折。"三个听完,认为有道理,便跟甲一起,坐在地上嚎啕⑦大哭起来。

有位老太太见此情景,连忙上前询问,当她弄清原因后,也呜呜地大哭不止。四人忙问:"你为什么也要哭啊?"

---

① 诗友:经常写诗唱和的朋友。Fellow literature lovers.
② 不由:控制不住,忍不住。Cannot but.
③ 吟:吟咏作诗。Chant, compose (poetry).
④ 云:说。Say.
⑤ 出口成章:话说出口就是一篇文章,形容文思敏捷,谈吐风雅。Talk easily with adroit phrases.
⑥ 绝顶:非常,极。Extremely.
⑦ 嚎啕:大声哭。Cry loudly, wail.

老太太悲伤地说:"我是担心把自己的肠子笑断。"

55. Ludicrous Pretension

There were four scholars, A, B, C, D, who all liked to write poems, and so they became literary cronies.

One day, the four went for a spring outing together to the suburbs. When they saw a pagoda standing on the other side of a river they instantly got into a poetic mood, and each composed a line of a poem.

A: From afar, I spy a pagoda.

B: Looking closely, it surely is a pagoda.

C: The more I look at it, the more it is like a pagoda.

D: It is a pagoda, after all.

When they finished, they heaped praises upon one another. Then suddenly A said to his pals: "The ancients said, 'Those endowed with cleverness cannot enjoy longevity.' As we four can write fine poems spontaneously, we are of course the cleverest people and therefore it seems we'll surely die young." The others thought he was right, and so, sitting on the ground, they all wailed loudly.

An old lady saw this and came over to ask why. When she learned the reason, she also wailed loudly. The four hastened to ask: "Why are you crying too?"

The old lady said sadly: "I was worried that I would laugh so hard that my stomach would burst."

56. 靶子神助阵

古时候,有员武将领兵去打仗,眼看就要被打败的时候,忽然天降神兵,前来助阵,结果反败为胜。

取胜之后,这员武将连忙趴在地上磕头①,叩问② 神的姓名。神回答说:"我是靶子神。"

武将又连着磕了几个响头③,不胜感激地问道:"小将有何功德④,敢烦尊神前来助阵?"

靶子神回答说:"我感谢你平时在校场⑤上练习射箭时,从来没有一箭射伤过我。"

56. Help From the
God of the Target

In ancient times there was an incompetent general who once led his soldiers out to a battle. Just as they were about to be defeated, some troops from Heaven led by a god suddenly came to their help and turned the tide of battle.

---

① 磕头:旧时礼节,跪在地上两手扶地,头挨地。Kowtow.
② 叩问:询问。Inquire
③ 响头:磕头时俯头着地发出声音,形容态度诚恳。Very sincere kowtow.
④ 功德:功业和恩德。Credits and virtues.
⑤ 校场:旧时操练、演习或比武的地方。Drilling ground.

Right after the victory the general hastily knelt down on the ground, kowtowed, and asked the god's name. The god said, "I am the God of the Target."

The general kowtowed again and again earnestly, and asked gratefully: "What merits do I have to deserve your help?"

The God of the Target said, "I wanted to thank you because when you practice shooting on the drilling ground you have never hurt me with a single shot."

57. 笑话一担

有一秀才在七十岁时,忽生一子,便取名叫"年纪"。一年以后,又生了,看模样①像是读书的材料②,便取名叫"学问"。第三年又生一子,自己也不禁③好笑:"如此年纪,还生此儿,真是笑话。"便取名叫"笑话"。

三个孩子长大后,都不成器④,只好让他们上山打柴。一天,他们打柴归来,秀才问:"三人中谁打的柴多?"

---

① 模样:情势、样子、情况。The way someone or something looks.
② 材料:比喻适合做某事的人才。Material.
③ 不禁:克制不住,忍不住。Can't refrain from.
④ 成器:比喻成为有用的人。Become a useful person.

秀才妻子回答说:"'年纪'有一把①,'学问'一点也无,'笑话'倒有一担。"

57. A Load of Jokes

A scholar was almost seventy years old when he had a baby son, so he named his son "Age". Before long, he had another son who seemed to have the makings of a scholar and thus was named "Learning". The following year, he had a third son.

He thought, "It's quite a joke to have a son at such an advanced age." So he called the little one "Joke".

When the three kids grew up they were all good for nothing. One day the scholar told them to gather firewood in the mountains. After they returned home he asked, "Which of the three has got the most firewood?"

His wife answered, "As for Age, there is a bunch. As for Learning, there is none. But as for Joke, there is a whole load."

---

① 一把:"把"为量词;一把,这里指年纪大。Bunch, handful.

58. 死了一千年

一个门客①不知怎样巴结②贵人才好。

一天,他对贵人说:"我昨天晚上做了个梦,梦见

---

　　① 门客:官僚贵族家中养的帮闲或帮忙的人。A retainer or advisor employed at an official's home.
　　② 巴结:奉承讨好。Fawn on.

您活了一千年。"

贵人道:"梦总是和实情相反。我听说,梦见生就要死,你的梦大概有些不吉祥吧?"

那门客马上改口①道:"呸! 我真混,竟说错了。我其实是梦见您死了一千年。"

58. Dead for a Thousand Years

A retainer was very eager to curry favor with his master.

One day he said to him:"I dreamt last night that you had lived for a thousand years."

The master said, "Dreams always tell the opposite. I heard that birth in a dream means death in reality. Maybe your dream was not auspicious."

The retainer quickly corrected himself:"Ah, how stupid of me! Actually I dreamt that you had been dead for a thousand years."

---

① 改口:改变说话的内容或口气。Correct oneself.

59. 老虎暂时过境

唐朝大历年间①,荆州有个叫冯希乐的人,很会阿谀奉承②,溜须拍马③。

有一次,他去拜见县令,县令留他喝酒。他吹捧县令说:"您把贵县治理得天下无比④,我这一路走来,老百姓无不异口同声⑤地称赞您的功德,连那吃人的老虎也被您感化得离开了县境!"

他的话音刚落,忽然有个衙役跑进来禀报⑥:"老爷,昨天晚上,本县张家庄又有两个人被老虎吃掉。"

当县令问冯希乐是怎么回事时,冯希乐回答说:"这一定是老虎暂时从贵县经过!"

---

① 大历年间:766—779 年,唐代宗李豫的年号。Reign period (766—779) of Emperor Daizong of the Tang Dynasty.

② 阿谀奉承:曲意谄媚迎合他人。Flatter and toady to.

③ 溜须拍马:比喻谄媚奉承。Lick somebody's boots.

④ 天下无比:独一无二,天下没有可以比拟的。Without equal, peerless.

⑤ 异口同声:很多人说同样的话,形容众口一辞。With one voice.

⑥ 禀报:指向上级或长辈报告。Report (to one's superior).

59. The Tiger Was Just Passing Through

In the Dali reign period of the Tang Dynasty there was a man called Feng Xile in Jinzhou who was a shameless flatterer.

Once he went to pay the county governor a formal visit and was invited in for a drink. He said to the governor flatteringly: "The county under your administration is beyond comparison. All along the way here I heard people praising your virtues and accomplishments. Even the fierce tigers have been moved by your kindness and have left the county."

He had barely finished saying this when a messenger rushed in to report: "Last night two more people were eaten by a tiger, sir."

The county governor then asked Feng to explain. Feng Xile replied, "It must have been a strange tiger that was passing through our county."

60. 臭味才来

某清客①善于拍马②奉承。

一天，主人放了个屁。他听见后，故意问道："什么响了一下？"

主人说："我放了个屁。"

清客说："不臭，不臭！"

主人说："好人的屁应当是臭的，要不臭就不好了。"

清客马上用手在自己鼻子前扇了扇，说："臭味才来，才来。"

60. The Bad Smell Has Just Arrived

Once at an aristocrat's home there was a literary man employed there who was especially adept at toadying.

One day the aristocrat broke wind. The literary man heard it but asked deliberately："What sound is that?" The aristocrat said："I farted. " The

---

① 清客：旧时在显贵人家帮闲的门客。A literary man employed as an advisor at an aristocrat's home.
② 拍马：向人谄媚。Toady to.

144

man said fawningly: "It doesn't smell. No smell at all!"

The aristocrat said, "When good people break wind, it should smell bad. Otherwise, it's not right."

The literary man immediately fanned his nose with his hand and said: "The smell has just arrived, just arrived."

61. 相法^①不准

有人问一相面^②人说："你的相法，向来灵验^③，为什么现在却不灵了呢？"

相面人皱皱眉头说："现在相面和过去有所不同：从前凡遇上方面大耳的，必定富贵^④；现在遇上方面大耳的，反而落寞^⑤；只有尖头尖嘴的，专会钻营取巧的，倒富贵起来。这叫我如何相得准呢？"

61. Can't Tell Fortunes Any More

Someone asked a fortune teller: "You could always tell people's fortunes by reading their faces before. But how come you can't do that any more?"

The fortune teller frowned and said: "Nowadays things are different. In the past when people with big heads and square faces came you could be

---

① 相法：指根据人的面相、气色等推断吉凶祸福的本领。Ability to tell a fortune.
② 相面：指观察人的相貌来推测吉凶。Practice physiognomy.
③ 灵验：指能得到印证。Right.
④ 富贵：指有钱有势。Wealth and power.
⑤ 落寞：冷落凄凉，落魄。Down and out, desolate.

sure that they had both wealth and rank. But now such people are down and out. In contrast, only those with bullet heads and pouting mouths who are specially good at flattering and fawning can get rich and powerful. How can I tell their fortunes properly?"

62. 牡牛肚子

有个财主嘱咐自己的仆人说:"你们跟着我出门,应见机行事,该说大话①的时候就得说几句大话,也好装装我的门面②。"仆人听了,连连点点表示答应。

头天③晚上,他们住进一座道观,正好听见一个道士说三清殿④如何如何大。没等那道士说完,仆人就说:"你说来说去,那三清殿也只不过同我家老爷的正房⑤一样大!"财主听了,高兴地点了点头。

第二晚上,他们住进一家旅馆,正好听见一位旅客说龙船⑥如何如何大。没等那位旅客说完,仆人就又说:"你说来说去,那龙船也只不过同我家老爷的帐船⑦一样大!"财主听了,得意地笑了笑。

第三天晚上,他们住进一户农家,正好听见一个庄稼人说牡牛⑧的肚子如何如何大。没等那个庄稼

---

① 大话:虚夸的话。Big talk.
② 门面:指商店房屋临街的一面。比喻外表、表面。Shop front; appearance.
③ 头天:第一天。The first day.
④ 三清殿:道教宫观。道家认为人天两界之外,另有三清,为神仙居住的地方。The Sanqing Hall, where Daoist priests believe the immortals live, in contrast to the world of humans and Heaven.
⑤ 正房:指座北朝南的正面房屋。Principal rooms.
⑥ 龙船:装饰成龙形的细长的船。Dragon boat.
⑦ 帐船:装饰有帐幔的游船。A boat with an awning.
⑧ 牡牛:公牛。Bull.

148

人说完,仆人抢着说:"你说来说去,那牡牛的肚子也只不过同我家老爷的肚子一般大!"财主听了,气得大肚子一鼓一鼓的。

62. A Bull's Belly

A rich man once instructed his servant:"When you are out with me, you should act according to circumstances and talk big whenever appropriate so as to create a good public image." The servant nodded his head repeatedly in compliance.

One night they put up at a Daoist temple, where they heard a Daoist priest talking about how large the Sanqing Hall was. Hardly had the priest finished his tale when the servant said, "No matter how large you say it is, it's only as big as the main room in our master's house!" The rich man nodded in delight.

On the next night they checked in at a hotel and happened to hear a customer saying how large the dragon-boat was. Before the man finished, the servant cut in boastfully: "No matter how large you say it is, it's no bigger than our master's boat!" Hearing this, the rich man smirked.

On the third night they stayed at a farmer's house. When the host talked about how big his bull's belly was, the servant quickly blurted out: "No matter how large you say it is, it can't be as big as our master's belly!" The rich man became so infuriated at this that his big belly almost burst with anger.

63. 夸富

一个人对客人夸口说："我家是应有尽有。"说完，伸出两个手指，又说："所少的，只是天上的太阳和月亮。"话还没说完，儿子出来说："厨房没有柴禾了。"那个人又伸出一个手指接着说："对，对，还有柴禾。"

63. Boasting of Riches

A host was boasting to his guests: "I have everything in my house," while holding out two fingers: "Except for the sun and the moon in the sky." He had no sooner finished than his son rushed in and said, "There's no firewood in the kitchen." The host instantly stuck out another finger and said: "Yes, yes, and firewood."

64. 山灰蚊肝

甲乙二人相遇,脸上都显出不高兴的样子。乙问甲:"请问老兄,你为什么不高兴呢?"

甲说:"我虽身居中国①,耳却能听万里。我刚才静坐时,因听见西天②有一个和尚,在那里诵经,我嫌聒噪③,喝令他别再念了,那和尚不理睬我,还是照念,我一气之下,就把一座须弥山④拿在手里,当一石块扔去撞他。谁料那和尚,等山坠⑤下来的时候,他只把眼睛一闭,用手抹一抹,口里说道:'哪里飘来的砂灰,几乎眯⑥了我的眼睛。'说完照旧去念经。好像从未打着他似的,使我对他一点办法也没有,你说气人不气人。"说完又问乙:"请问老兄你为什么脸上也不高兴呢?"

乙说:"昨天,有一客人到我家来,没什么好东西

---

① 中国:上古时代,我国华夏族建国于黄河流域,以为居天下之中,故称中国。后泛指中原地区。Ancient Chinese people established in the Yellow River valley a country, 中国, deeming it the center of the world. Later 中国 also referred to the area of the middle and lower reaches of the Yellow River.
② 西天:我国佛教徒称佛祖所在之处。The West, where the Buddhists believe the Buddhist patriarch was.
③ 聒(guō)噪:方言。指大声吵闹。(Dialect) noisy, boisterous.
④ 须弥山:佛教传说中的山名。The legendary Mount Xumi (Buddhist).
⑤ 坠:落下,掉下。Fall.
⑥ 眯(mi):灰沙等杂物进到眼里,使眼不能睁开看东西。Get into one's eyes.

款待他，我便捉了一只蚊子，剖开它的肚子，取出它的心肝，用刀切成一百二十块，下锅炒熟。谁知客人吃下蚊肝后，噎①在嗓子里不上不下，直②埋怨我把肝切大了，现在还睡在我家里哼个不住，你说气人不气人。"

甲说："天下人中哪有这么细的嗓子？"

---

① 噎 yē：食物堵住了喉咙。Choke.
② 直：不断地。Continuously.

154

乙说:"你既然有能够听西天和尚诵经的耳朵,容得下须弥山的大眼睛,难道就不许我有让蚊子心肝噎住这么细的嗓子吗?"

64. Mountain-Sized Duot and Mosquito's Liver

Two men, A and B, met, both looking unhappy. B asked A:"Won't you please tell me why you are so unhappy?"

A answered, "Although I am in the center of the world, I can hear what happens far away. I was sitting still when I heard a monk chanting in the west. Since he made so much noise, I told him to stop. But he paid no heed and carried on. I was so angry that I uprooted Mount Xumi and threw it at him. But the monk, just as the mountain fell on him, only closed and then wiped his eyes, saying, "Where did that piece of dust come from?" Then he went on with his chanting as if nothing had happened. There was nothing I could do about it, so how could I not get angry?" He then asked B: "Why are you so unhappy?"

B said, "Yesterday, a guest dropped in. As I had nothing better to entertain him with, I caught a mosquito, cut open its belly, took out its liver, cut it into 120 pieces and stir-fried it. But the guest choked on the mosquito's liver, complaining that the pieces were too big. He is still lying in my house, groaning all day long. How can I not be annoyed?"

A said, "How can a person have such a narrow throat?"

B retorted, "If you have ears that can hear a monk chanting in the west, and if there is a monk whose eyes are even bigger than Mount Xumi, how can there not be a person with such a narrow throat that he chokes on a mosquito's liver?"

65. 梦见孔子

有位教书先生在大白天睡觉。醒来以后,他自觉无趣,便对学生撒谎说:"我刚才梦见了孔子①,所以多睡了一会。"

第二天白天,有个弟子②也学着他的样,在课堂上睡起觉来。这位先生一见非常恼火,用戒尺③把他敲醒,怒气冲冲地责问他:"你怎么也在大白天睡起觉来?"

这个弟子连忙辩解说:"我刚才也梦见孔子了,所以没敢醒!"

先生听后问他:"你既然也梦见了孔子,那你就给我说,孔子对你讲了些什么?"

弟子做了个鬼脸说:"孔子亲口对我讲,他昨天并没有会见您!"

---

① 孔子:公元前551—前479年,春秋末期思想家、政治家、教育家,儒家的创始人。Confucius (551 BC—479 BC), philosopher, educationist, politician and founder of Confucianism.
② 弟子:学生、门徒。Student, disciple.
③ 戒尺:旧时老师对学生施行体罚时所用的木板。Teacher's stick (for punishing pupils).

65. Dreaming of Confucius

A schoolmaster once dozed off during the day. After he woke up he felt embarrassed and so told his students a lie: "Just now I dreamt about Confucius, so I kept sleeping for a while."

The next day, a student followed suit by dozing off during class. The schoolmaster was very angry and, hitting him up with his stick, asked him in a rage: "How could you go to sleep in broad daylight?"

The student hastened to explain: "I dreamt about Confucius just now, so I didn't dare to wake up."

The master asked him: "If you dreamt about Confucius, too, then tell me what Confucius told you just now."

Grimacing, the student replied, "He told me that he didn't meet you yesterday."

66. 胡须上的被子

有个人家里穷得用草垫当被子,而他的儿子又偏偏是个实打实①的人,家中有什么都如实地告诉别人。

有一天,这个人教育儿子说:"如果有人问咱家睡觉盖的什么,你就说盖的是被子。"

---

① 实打实:实实在在。Honest, true.

第二天起床后,这人出来陪伴客人,有一根草粘在胡须上。儿子在旁边看见,忙大声喊道:"爹！爹！你怎么不把胡须上的那条被子拂①掉！"

66. Quilted Beard

A man was so poor that he had to use a straw mattress as a quilt. His son was very honest who would tell people everything about his family.

One day the man told his son: "If someone asks you what we cover ourselves with at night, just tell him that we use a quilt."

The next day, right after they got up, the man went out to entertain a guest, not noticing that he had a piece of straw in his beard. Seeing this, his son shouted loudly: "Dad, Dad, why don't you take the quilt out of your beard?"

---

① 拂(fú):拂拭,抖落。Whisk.

67. 菩萨①打架

从前有个人非常迷信,在家里供奉了许多菩萨。

一天,他出门办事,临走时一再叮嘱儿子:"等一会儿锅里的肉煮好了,先供奉菩萨,千万不要忘记了。"

父亲走后,儿子不仅把煮好的肉吃了个精光,而且还把菩萨打了个稀巴烂②。

父亲回到家里,一见此情此景,怒气冲冲地问儿子:"这些菩萨是谁打碎的?"

"刚才他们为了争肉吃,互相打了起来,一个个打得粉身碎骨。"儿子不慌不忙地说。

"胡说! 菩萨是泥做的,怎么会自个③打起来?"父亲大声叱斥说。

这时,儿子指着打碎的菩萨说:"既然它们是泥做的,又怎么会吃肉呢?"

67. Fighting Buddhas

A man who was very superstitious enshrined

---

① 菩萨:佛教指修行到了较高程度,仅次于佛的人。(Here) Buddha.
② 稀巴烂:指很破碎,很烂。Shattered.
③ 自个:方言。自己。(Dialect) oneself.

and worshipped many statues of Buddha in his home.

One day, just before he went out on business, he told his son again and again: "When the meat in the pot is ready, don't forget to serve the Buddhas first."

After his father had left the son not only ate all the meat, he also smashed the Buddhas to pieces.

When his father got home and saw this, he

163

asked his son furiously: "Who smashed the Buddhas?"

"Just now they fought over the meat and smashed each other to pieces," the son said calmly.

"Nonsense! The Buddhas are all made of clay. How can they fight each other?" the father scolded him loudly.

Then, pointing to the broken Buddhas, the son said, "If they are made of clay, how could they eat meat?"

68. 酷信风水①

从前有个人酷信风水,不论做什么事,事先总要问问风水先生,风水先生怎么说,他就怎么去做。家里人对此很反感,但又拿他没办法。

有一天,他闲着没事,坐在墙根底下晒太阳。忽然,墙被一阵狂风刮倒,把他压在了下面。他挣扎不得,只好连声呼喊:"救命啊! 救命啊!"

儿子听见喊声,连忙从家里赶来。一看是父亲被倒塌的墙压住了,儿子不慌不忙地对他说:"您先忍一会儿,等我去问问风水先生,看看今儿个②能不能动土。"

68. Believer in Geomancy

Once there was an extremely superstitious man who wouldn't do anything without consulting a geomancer, following his advice to the letter. His family members were disgusted with him, but could do nothing about it.

---

① 风水:旧指宅基地、坟地等的地脉、山水方向。风水先生就是以看风水等为职业的人。Geomantic omen read by a geomancer.
② 今儿个:今天。Today.

One day he was sunning himself idly against a wall, which suddenly fell upon him in a wild gust of wind. He struggled desperately but couldn't get up, and so had to cry out: "Help! Help!"

Hearing the cry, his son rushed out of the house. When he saw it was his father who was under the fallen wall, he said deliberately: "Just hold on for a while. Let me go and ask the geomancer first and see if it's proper to move the bricks today."

69. 怕老婆

甲和乙两个人都非常怕老婆。老婆叫他们往东，他们不敢朝西；老婆叫他们打狗，他们不敢打鸡。

有一天，乙到甲家对甲诉苦说："我老婆近来对我管得更狠了，到晚上连尿盆也要我来端。"

甲听了愤愤不平，又是挽袖子、又是伸胳膊地说："这事有什么难的，要是我……"

甲的话还没有说完，他的老婆就在背后厉声喝道："要是你又能怎样？"

甲一听老婆的口气①不对，连忙跪在地上说："要是我，我就马上去端。"

69. Henpecked Husbands

Mr A and Mr B were both henpecked. When their wives told them to go east, they wouldn't dare go west.

One day Mr B poured out his woes to Mr A: "My wife has been getting more bossy with me recently. She even tells me to take the chamber pot

---

① 口气：指说话的气势或感情色彩。Tone.

to her at night. "

Mr A felt indignant and, stretching out his arms while rolling up his sleeves, he said: "If I were you..."

But before he could finish, his wife shouted harshly behind him: "What would you do if you were him?"

Seeing that his wife was angry again, Mr A hurriedly knelt down and said: "If I were him, I would take the chamber pot right away. "

70. 说话算数

有个人像老鼠怕猫一样地害怕老婆。有一天晚上，他由于端尿盆慢了一点，又被老婆揪住头发猛打。打得他实在无法忍受，只好钻到了床下面。

他老婆见他一反常态，心里更加恼火，于是在床边跺着脚说："你快点给我滚出来！不然我就……"

还没等老婆把话说完，只听那人在床下面嗫嗫嚅嚅①地说："大丈夫②说话算数，我说不出去，就是不出去！"

70. Words That Count

A man was afraid of his wife as much as a mouse is scared of a cat. One night, as he was a bit slow in taking his wife the chamber pot, the woman grabbed him by the hair and slapped him fiercely until he really couldn't bear it and slipped under the bed.

Seeing that he was not as obedient as usual,

---

① 嗫(niè)嗫嚅(rú)嚅：想说话而又不敢说，吞吞吐吐。Speak haltingly.
② 大丈夫：指有气节、有作为的男子。A true man, a real man.

his wife became even more irritated. She stamped her feet and shouted: "Come out from under the bed now, or I'll..."

The man said in a trembling voice: "A man's words count. I say I won't come out and I simply will not!"

71. 母猪肉

有个卖母猪肉①的,深怕别人知道了不买,便再三嘱咐他儿子不要说是母猪肉。过了一会儿,来了个买肉的。他儿子上前便道:"我家卖的可不是母猪肉呀!"来人觉得不对头,扭头就走了。父亲十分生气,怒冲冲地说:"我已经嘱咐过你,你怎么反倒先告诉人家!"于是把儿子揍了一顿。

过了片刻,又来了一个买主,问道:"这肉皮那么厚,莫非是母猪肉?"

---

① 母猪肉:指作种猪用的母猪,其皮厚,肉煮不烂,不能食用。
A sow's skin is normally thick and its meat is hard to boil.

儿子这时幸灾乐祸①地对父亲说："你看怎么样？难道这句话也是我说起的吗？"

71. Sow's Meat

A man who sold sow's meat dreaded most that people would not buy the meat if they knew the truth, so he told his son over and over again never to say the meat came from sows.

Before long a customer came. His son told him eagerly："The meat we have is not from a sow." The customer felt there was something fishy about this and so he went away. The father was very angry and said, "I told you before. Why did you mention it first?" So he gave the boy a sound beating.

A little while later, another customer came and asked："That pig's skin is too thick. It must be a sow."

The son took great pleasure in this and said to his father："Look, I didn't mention it first this time."

---

① 幸灾乐祸：指看见别人遭到灾祸反而高兴。Gloat over others' misfortune.

172

72. 怕馒头

有一个穷书生想吃馒头，可是没钱买。这天他走到市场上，见店铺前摆着好多馒头，便大叫一声，昏倒在地。馒头铺的主人感到很惊奇，忙问他是怎么回事。书生道："我怕馒头。"主人道："世上哪有怕馒头的道理！"便在一间空屋子里放上百余个馒头，然后把书生关在屋里。他自己躲在屋外，悄悄等着看会发生什么事。

过了半天,也没有听到屋里有什么异常的动静,店主人便从门缝中向屋里张望,只见穷书生用手抓着馒头,狼吞虎咽①,已经把馒头吃了一半。主人赶忙打开门,问他是什么缘故。书生道:"我见那么多馒头摆在屋里,不知怎么回事,忽然不怕它了。"

主人这才知道受了骗,生气地斥问道:"你现在还有什么可怕的吗?"

书生道:"现在我怕的是香茶两碗!"

72. Scared of Steamed Bread

A poor student wanted very much to eat steamed bread, but just couldn't afford it.

One day he went to the market and saw a lot of steamed bread in front of a bread store. He gave a wild cry and fell to the ground. The store owner was greatly surprised and hastened to ask him what was wrong. The student replied, "The steamed bread scared me." The store owner said, "How can anyone be afraid of steamed bread?" He then put over 100 pieces of steamed bread in an empty room and let the student stay in it. He then

---

① 狼吞虎咽:形容吃东西极其急猛的样子。Gobble down.

hid outside to see what would happen.

After quite a while he still had not heard anything strange in the room, so he peeped in through a crack in the door. He saw the student wolfing down steamed bread. Half of the steamed bread in the room had already disappeared. Hurriedly he opened the door and asked the student: "What is the matter?" The student replied, "When I saw so much steamed bread in the room for some reason I suddenly was not afraid of it any more."

The store owner realized that he had been taken in, so he chided the student angrily: "Are you scared of anything now?"

The student replied, "Now I'm scared of two cups of fragrant tea!"

73. 占把椅子坐

有一家来了不少讨债的,屋里椅子凳子全坐满了,有的只好坐在门槛①上。主人便悄悄对坐在门槛上的说:"您明天可以早来一会儿。"那人暗忖②,一定是先把自己的债务了结③,心中万分高兴,便张罗④着让其他债主们先回家。

第二天一大早,这人便兴冲冲地赶来讨债。他一见主人,就说:"您约我今日早来,想必是先还我的钱吧?"主人摇了摇头,抱歉地说:"昨日招待不周,让您坐在门槛上,我心里甚⑤感不安,今天让您早来,可以先占把椅子来坐了。"

73. Occupying a Seat

Once a group of creditors came to a debtor's family. As all the chairs and stools were occupied, one of them had to sit on the threshold. The host said quietly to that creditor:"You should come ear-

---

① 门槛(kǎn):门框下端的横木。Threshold.
②ˈ 暗忖(cǔn):私下揣度、思量。Think.
③ 了结:解决,结束。Solve, end.
④ 张罗:安排。Arrange.
⑤ 甚:非常,十分,很。Very.

lier tomorrow." The man thought that the host wanted to pay him back his debt first, so, greatly delighted, he urged the other creditors to go home.

Early the next morning the creditor came happily to the debtor's home. As soon as he saw the host, he said, "You told me to come earlier today, so you must have planned to return my money first?" The host shook his head and apologized: "I was very sorry that you were poorly entertained yesterday and had to sit on the threshold. So I asked you to come earlier today so that you could occupy a seat first. "

74. 驴请假

胡趱喜爱下棋,常骑毛驴到别人家去下,早去晚归,日日如此。每当他到后,这家主人都吩咐家童把驴牵到后院喂好。胡趱对主人的照顾十分感谢。

一天,正下着棋,宫中①突然召胡趱回去,他急忙奔向后院牵驴,正看见毛驴喘息流汗,这家家童正从驴背上卸套。胡趱一看,明白了是怎么回事。

第二天又去下棋,主人又要让家童去喂驴,胡趱说:"不用了,今日没骑来。"

"为什么?"主人诧异地问。

胡趱说:"只因昨日回去,驴便头晕恶心,病倒了,今日向您请假,休息一下。"

主人听罢,羞得满脸通红。

74. Donkey on Leave

Hu Zan was fond of playing chess so much that every day he would ride on his donkey to a friend's home to play, and return home late. Each time he arrived the host would tell his servant to

---

① 宫中:指皇宫之中。The royal palace.

take the donkey into the backyard and feed it. Hu
Zan was very grateful for this.

One day when he was again playing chess,
there suddenly came a call from the emperor for
him to go to the palace. He hurried into the backyard to get his donkey, and there saw it panting
and covered in sweat while the servant was taking
off the harness. He realized what had happened at
once.

180

The next day he went to play chess as usual, and again the host told his servant to feed the donkey. Hu Zan said, "No, please don't bother. I didn't come on it today."

"But why?" The host asked in surprise.

"Because," Hu Zan replied, "when we got home yesterday the donkey had a headache and felt sick. It has asked you for leave today so that it can take a rest." The host blushed with embarrassment.

75. 误装门闩①

有个木匠给人家安装门闩时,误把门闩装在了门外边。这家主人一见,气得暴跳如雷地骂道:"难道你的眼瞎啦!"

① 门闩(shuān):插在关上的门背后、使门开不了的杠子。Door bolt.

木匠回骂①道:"你的眼才真正瞎了呢?"

主人说:"你凭什么说我的眼瞎了?"

木匠回答说:"你要是眼不瞎,为啥叫我这个木匠来给你家干活!"

75. Misplaced Door Bolt

Once a carpenter tried to fix a bolt for a house door, but placed it on the outside of the door instead of the inside. Seeing this, the house owner flew into a rage and shouted:"Are you blind?"

The carpenter retorted:"It is you who are blind."

The house owner said:"How can you say that I'm blind?"

The carpenter responded, "If you are not blind, why did you ask a carpenter like me to work for you?"

---

① 回骂:反骂。Retort.

76. 静坐有益

有位禅师①对一个信徒说："参禅②时，一定要闭目静坐，杜绝万念。"

这个信徒按照禅师的嘱咐，天天坚持参禅静坐。有一天夜里，坐到五更③时，突然想起过去有人借过

---

① 禅师：对和尚的尊称。A respectful form of address for a monk.

② 参禅：佛教指静坐冥想，领悟佛理。Meditate.

③ 五更：旧时把一夜分为五更，五更就是天亮之前。The night was formerly divided into five two-hour periods. 五更 is the last one before dawn.

184

他一斗麦子，至今未还。于是他连忙把老婆喊醒，高兴地对老婆说："禅师教我静坐果然有益，要不然，这一斗麦子被人家骗去了。"

76. It Pays to Meditate

A Buddhist monk once told a Buddhist layman："When you are meditating you must close your eyes and sit quietly without a trace of any distracting thought. "

The layman did sit quietly every day in meditation as the monk told him. One night he sat up until almost dawn，when suddenly it came to him that somebody had once borrowed from him a *dou* of wheat. So he hurried to wake up his wife and told her delightedly："It really pays to sit quietly，as the monk said. Otherwise，we would have been cheated out of a *dou* of wheat. "

77. 长生丹药

一个医生得了重病。他自知性命难保，便在枕头上大喊大叫："如果哪位医生能替我把病治好，我现在有长生丹药回谢他，叫他吃了长命百岁。"

77. Longevity Pills

A doctor fell seriously ill. Knowing that he did not have much time left, he shouted from his bed: "If any doctor can get rid of my illness I will give him some longevity pills so that he can live a long life."

78. 年糕是馊①的

有个小贩在叫卖年糕时,声音特别小,连三步之外都听不到。旁边站着的人见了,觉得很奇怪,便笑着问他:"你为什么不大点声儿叫卖呢?"

那小贩低声回答说:"我饿了,浑身没有一点劲。"

"既然饿了,为什么不吃几块年糕?"旁边站着的人又问道。

那小贩仍有气无力地回答说:"你们不知道,我这些年糕全是馊的!"

78. Stale Cakes

A peddler of New Year cakes was hawking his wares, but his voice was so low that he could hardly be heard even a few steps away. Someone nearby thought this was strange, and asked him, laughing:"Why don't you raise your voice if you want to sell your cakes?"

The peddler answered in a feeble voice:"I'm

---

① 馊:饭菜等因变质而发出酸臭味。Sour, stale.

年 糕

starved and have no strength. "

"Then why don't you eat a few of your cakes?" the man asked.

The peddler moaned, "You don't understand. These cakes are all stale. "

79. 开天窗

有个人专门讨便宜①,凡是亲朋有事,他就出头敛份子②钱,可自己那 份却经常隐瞒不出,并把剩余的钱装入自己腰包③。

阎王④恨他心黑手狠,便把他捉到阴间⑤,命关在黑牢里受罪。他一进牢门,就高喊说:"这个屋子黑得很,现在有几个人在这里,咱们快敛个份子开个天窗,也好明亮明亮。"

79. Open a Skylight

There was a man who always sought undue advantages. Whenever his relatives or friends had any financial problems he would act as a collector to club together the money needed to help them. But he seldom paid his share, and always put any remaining cash into his own pocket.

---

① 便宜(piányi):不该得到的利益。Unmerited advantages.
② 份子:集体送礼时每人分摊的钱,泛指做礼物的现钱。One's share of expenses for a gift.
③ 腰包:随身带的钱包。Purse, pocket.
④ 阎王:佛教称主管地狱的神。King of Hell (Buddhist).
⑤ 阴间:迷信指人死后灵魂所在的地方。Hell.

.The King of Hell hated such a wicked man.
He dragged him down to the nether world and put
him into a dark dungeon to suffer. But the first
thing the man did was to shout, "This room is too
dark. Since we have several people here, let's collect some money to get a skylight installed."

190

80. 贫士装阔

从前有个读书人，家里穷得叮当响①，平时在别人面前，却偏偏爱装阔。

有个小偷信以为真，便在一天夜里到他家去偷东西。可是读书人屋子里空空荡荡，没有什么东西可偷，小偷才知道自己受了骗，上了当，只好一边骂着，一边往外走。

读书人听见小偷的骂人话，连忙把枕头底下仅有的几文钱摸出来，追上去送给了小偷，并苦苦哀求小偷说："您这次光顾寒舍②，照顾极不周到，希望您能多多包涵，以后千万不要在别人面前说我家里穷得什么也没有啊！"

80. Pretending to Be Rich

A certain scholar was as poor as a church mouse but liked to pretend he was rich to other people.

A thief believed that he was really rich, and

---

① 叮当响：锅、盘、碗撞击的声音，形象地指什么也没有。Sounds of pots and pans, meaning emptiness.
② 寒舍：对别人谦称自己的家。My humble house.

so broke into his house one night. But when he saw that the scholar's house was almost empty and didn't have anything to steal, he realized that he had been fooled, and cursed the man as he went out.

Hearing the thief's curses, the scholar quickly

fished out from under his pillow the few pennies he had. He caught up with the thief and, presenting the pennies to him, begged, "Excuse me for not being able to receive you properly at my humble home. Please be sure not to tell people that I haven't got anything valuable."

81. 让它到邻居家去疼

从前有个人,脚上长了一个恶疮,疼得他呼爹喊娘。

有一天,他疼得实在受不了,便对家里人说:"你们赶快给我在后墙上凿个洞。"家里人不解其意①便按他的吩咐,在后墙凿起来。

洞凿成以后,他连忙把那只长疮的脚伸进洞里,一直伸进一尺多。家里人疑惑不解②地问他:"您这是什么意思?"只听他洋洋自得③地回答说:"让它到邻居家去疼吧! 这下可与我无关了!"

81. Let the Pain Go to the Neighbors

A man had a bad boil on his foot, which caused him terrible pain.

One day when he just couldn't stand it any more he told his family:"Go quickly and bore a hole in the back wall." They did not understand

---

① 不解其意:不了解他的用意。Do not understand.
② 疑惑不解:怀疑、迷惑,不了解。Feel puzzled, have doubts.
③ 洋洋自得:形容自我欣赏,非常得意的样子。Complacently.

but just did as they were told.

When the hole was finished, the man thrust his aching foot into it. His family members were puzzled and asked him: "What do you mean by doing this?" He replied complacently: "Let the pain go to the neighbors; it has nothing to do with me now!"

82. 送您一个令尊①

有一次，一个庄稼人问一个秀才："平时常听人说'令尊'，这'令尊'是什么意思呢？"

秀才作弄②庄稼人说："这'令尊'二字，是用来称呼别人的儿子的。"秀才说完，偷偷地掩口而笑。

这个庄稼人信以为真，于是反问秀才说："那么，您有几个令尊呢？"

---

① 令尊：尊称对方的父亲。A respectful form of address for the father of the person spoken to.
② 作弄：即捉弄。故意开玩笑，使人为难。Poke fun at; make a fool of.

秀才一听,心里很恼火,但又不好当面发作,只好应付说:"我已经没有令尊了。"

庄稼人以为他真的没有儿子,便好心地安慰他说:"要是您没有令尊,也用不着伤心。我家里有四个,要是您愿意,就送一个做您的令尊吧!"

82. I'll Give You a Sire

Once a peasant asked a learned man:"I often hear people use the word 'sire'. What does it mean?"

The other man wanted to make fun of him, and said with a secret laugh:"This word is used to address the sons of other people."

The farmer believed him and asked the learned man:"How many sires do you have?"

Though much annoyed, the other did not dare to flare up. He had to stall him by saying, "I have no sires anymore."

The farmer believed he really had no sons, so he consoled him sympathetically:"If you haven't got any sires, you don't have to be so sad. Since I've got four at home, I'll give you a sire if you like."

83. 愁虑二百岁寿诞

　　有个老头，子孙满堂①，富贵兼全。一百岁生日那天，来祝寿的客人熙熙攘攘，十分热闹，老头却愁眉不展②，一个劲地唉声叹气。大家见他这样忧虑，于是问道："您如此全福③，还有什么不高兴的？"

---

　　① 满堂：指子孙众多。A full room of (posterity).
　　② 愁眉不展：由于忧愁双眉紧锁，形容心事重重的样子。With a worried frown.
　　③ 全福：指子孙满堂、富贵兼全的福气。All happiness (usually said to an elderly person).

老头说:"我什么都不愁,只愁我将来过二百岁生日时,来祝寿的人要成百上千,教我怎么记得清!"

83. 200th Birthday Worries

An old man had a great number of descendants, and enjoyed both riches and honor. On his 100th birthday his home was bustling with people for the celebrations. Yet the old man looked worried, with knitted brows and deep sighs. Seeing this, people said to him: "You've got everything you could want. Why should you feel unhappy?"

The old man replied: "I'm not worried about anything, except that on my 200th birthday, hundreds of people will come for the celebrations. How will I be able to remember all of them?"

84. 偷锄

　　有个人到衙门告状说:"小人明天丢了一张锄,求老爷追究。"

　　县官一听,奇怪地问:"你这刁民,明天丢了锄头,怎么昨天不来告状?"

　　旁边有个衙役听了不觉失笑①,县官看见后,马上判决说:"大胆奴才②,偷锄的一定是你,你偷锄干什么用,快给我从实招来!"

---

　　① 不觉失笑:不知不觉忍不住发笑。Cannot help laughing.
　　② 奴才:奴仆,家奴。Servant.

200

这个衙役一听，不假思索①地回答说："小人偷锄，是想锄掉那些糊涂虫!"

84. The Missing Hoe

A man went to the local government to report："I lost a hoe tomorrow. Please help me to find the thief."

The governor asked in surprise："You cunning man. If you lost a hoe tomorrow, why didn't you come to report it yesterday?"

Hearing this, an attendant nearby couldn't help laughing. The governor turned on him："You bold flunky! It must have been you who stole the hoe. Now tell me the truth, why did you steal the hoe?"

The attendant replied without thinking："The reason why your servant stole the hoe is to hoe up idiots!"

---

① 不假思索：用不着想。形容说话做事敏捷。Readily, without thinking.

85. 炒面

　　有个人背着一口袋炒面进城去卖。走到河边,见河面上已结了冰。这时,他走得又累又饿,想坐下吃些炒面充饥。可是炒面必须用水来拌,他就在冰上凿了个窟窿①,就把炒面倒了进去,谁知炒面倒进去就没了,随倒随散,这人只是一再叹惜,却弄不清究竟是怎么回事。

---

　　① 窟窿:孔,洞。Hole.

过了一会儿,水面平静,现出了他自己的面影。他一见,心中大怒,叫道:"原来是你偷了我的炒面,竟还不知足,胆敢仰脸看我!"说着,一巴掌朝水面打去。

接连打了几巴掌,河水变浑了,人影也没了。他不觉纳闷①道:"这贼刚才还在这里,怎么转眼就不见啦?"

85. Parched Flour

A man carried a sack of parched flour to sell in the market. On his way he saw a river whose surface was already frozen. By then he was both tired and hungry, so he sat down and tried to eat some of the parched flour. But it had to be mixed with water before he could eat it. Therefore, he chopped a hole in the ice and tipped the flour into the hole. But the flour just disappeared. The more he poured in, the more it disappeared. The man was puzzled.

After a while the water became calm and he saw reflected in it his own image. He flew into a

---

① 纳闷:因为疑惑而发闷。Feel puzzled, wonder.

rage at the sight, and shouted:"It is you who stole my parched flour. How shameless of you that you should have the nerve to look me in the face!" As he said this, he gave his reflection a slap.

After several slaps, the water turned turbid and the image was nowhere to be seen. The man felt puzzled and said, "The thief was here just now. How come he vanished so quickly?"

86. 给我滚

隋朝①有个叫柳真的,官做到洛阳令②,却整日迷迷糊糊,非常健忘。

曾有一个人犯了罪,按法律应该受杖刑③。柳真看完罪状,勃然大怒,喝叫着立刻行刑。差役们当即把犯人的衣服扒④下扔到院子里。柳真正要下令行杖,恰巧有一个客人来访,柳真便陪客人说话去了。

当时正是冬天,那个犯人光着膀子⑤冷得受不了,踧⑥着身子挪⑦到大堂⑧台阶上晒太阳。过了一会儿,又索性拾起棉袄披在身上。

没有多久,柳真送客人走出大堂,回来时,远远看见此人蹲在台阶上,大声喝道:"什么东西,敢在我大堂边上捉虱子! 给我滚!"

那犯人二话不说,穿上棉袄径自出门走了。

---

① 隋朝:朝代名,公元 581 年杨坚建立,公元 618 年灭亡,共历三帝,三十八年。The Sui Dynasty (581—618) was founded by Yang Jian. Three emperors reigned for a total of 38 years.
② 令:官名,县令。An official title, county governor.
③ 杖刑:旧时拷打的刑罚。A punishment in olden times.
④ 扒:剥、脱。Strip.
⑤ 光膀子:指赤裸上身。Topless.
⑥ 踧:缓慢地行动。Move slowly.
⑦ 挪:移动。Move.
⑧ 大堂:旧时官署中办事的厅堂。The main hall of a local government building.

86. Now Get Out

In the Sui Dynasty there was a county governor called Liu Zhen who was very muddleheaded and forgetful.

The governor once sentenced a man to death. The bailiffs at once stripped the clothes off the man and threw them in the courtyard. Just as Liu Zhen was about to give the order for execution, a guest arrived, and so the governor went off to talk with him.

As it was then winter the naked criminal could hardly stand the cold. He moved slowly to the door of the court room to get some sunshine. Shortly after, he picked up his cotton-padded jacket from the courtyard outside and put it on.

Before long, Liu Zhen walked out of the hall to see his guest off. Seeing the man squatting on the steps, he shouted :"Who dares to pick lice outside my court room? Get out of here at once!"

The criminal quickly put on the rest of his clothes and simply walked out off the courtyard.

87. 发誓戒酒

有个人嗜酒如命,每天从早到晚总是酒不离口、口不离酒,已经成了酒癖。当朋友们极力劝他戒酒时,他装出一副被迫无奈的样子说:"我本来打算戒,现在只因为小儿子出门没有回来,心中十分挂念,只好用酒来消愁,等小儿子回来以后,我一定听从大家的劝告,坚决把酒戒掉。"

朋友们说:"光这样说说不算数,只有赌咒我们才信。"

于是,他当着众朋友的面发誓说:"我的小儿子回来以后,如果我还不戒酒,那就叫大酒缸把我压死,小酒杯把我噎死,跌在酒池里把我泡死,掉到酒海里把我淹死,罚我生为酿酒之人,死做酒厂之鬼,在酒泉①之下,永世不得翻身!"

朋友们听了问他:"您儿子究竟到什么地方去了?"

他回答说:"到杏花村②给我打酒去了。"

---

① 酒泉:"酒"与"九"同音。九泉,即地下,亦指阴间。酒 is a homophone of 九, and 九泉 means the nether world.
② 杏花村:地名,以产酒闻名。Name of a place famous for its wine.

87. Swearing Off Drinking

There was a habitual drinker who never stopped drinking or talking about wine from morning till night. Once, when his friends tried to persuade him to stop drinking, he pretended to comply by saying: "I meant to quit drinking, but as my little son is away from home and not yet back, I'm very worried. I have to try to drink my worries away. When my little son's back, I'll take your advice and give up drinking for sure. "

His friends said: "That doesn't count. You have to swear before we will believe you. " So he vowed: "After my little son comes back, if I'm still addicted to drink, let me be crushed by a wine vat, choked to death by a wine cup, or drowned in a pool or ocean of wine. May I be made to work in a winery when I'm alive, and be a ghost in a winery after I die, and never be set free in the nether world of wine. "

Hearing this, his friends asked, "Where on earth did your son go?"

He replied, "He went to the Xinghua Village to get me some wine. "

88. 看戏

　　一个瞎子、一个聋子和一个跛子坐在一起看戏，他们一边看戏一边评论。

　　瞎子说："今天的戏，唱得很好，不过行头①不行。"

　　聋子说："那是因为你看不见，其实行头也很好，只可惜唱的声音太小了点。"

---

　　① 行头：戏曲演出时，演员所用的服装和道具。Costumes and paraphernalia.

跛子接着说："你们说的都不全面,其实今天的戏唱的声音不小,行头也不错,可惜就是戏台子搭得歪了些。"

88. At a Theater

Three people, one blind, one deaf and one lame, were at a theater attending an opera while making comments among themselves.

The blind person said, "In today's opera the singing is pretty good, but the costumes and props are rather poor."

The deaf one responded, "That's because you can't see. Actually the costumes are very good; only the voices are a bit too low."

The cripple added, "Neither of you have described it completely. The voices of the singers are not really low, and the costumes are good. The pity is that the stage is not straight."

89. 难道只值半个字

从前有个纨袴①子弟，用五百金②捐了一个监生③。但他孤陋寡闻，什么也不懂。当妻子劝他在国子监④好好读书时，他却反问妻子："读书又有什么好处？"

妻子回答说："一字值千金⑤，多读书多识字又有什么不好！"

他一听，怒不可遏，抬手就打了妻子两个耳刮子⑥，并且边打边骂："照你这么说，难道我这么大一个人，只值半个字的价钱不成！"

---

① 纨袴：用细绢做的裤子，这里借指穿着华美的富家子弟。Trousers made of fine silk, here referring to fops and dandies.

② 五百金：五百两金子。500 *liang* of gold.

③ 监生：明清两代称在国子监读书或取得进国子监读书资格的人。清代可以用捐纳的办法取得这种称号。Those who studied or acquired the right to study at the imperial college in the Ming and Qing dynasties. It was legal to buy such a title in the Qing Dynasty.

④ 国子监：中国封建王朝最高的教育管理机关和最高学府。The higher-education administration and institution in the old days.

⑤ 一字值千金：称誉文辞精妙，价值极高的文章诗词。这里借指读书的重要性。A word is worth a thousand *liang* of gold — praise of excellent writing and learning.

⑥ 耳刮子：即耳光。Box on the ear.

89. Am I Worth Only Half a Word?

Once there was a playboy who was very ignorant and shallow, but he bought his way into the Imperial College with 500 *liang* of gold. When his wife urged him to study hard at the college, he asked: "What's the benefit of studying?" His wife replied, "One word can be worth a thousand pieces of gold. There's nothing bad in knowing more words."

Flaring up at this, he gave his wife two boxes on the ear and cursed her: "Do you mean to say that an important man like me is worth only half a word?"

90. 找菱角①

有个山里人来到水乡,在一棵大树下闲坐。他见树下丢着一个菱角,拾起来便吃,觉得又甜又面,很是好吃,于是爬到树上,扳②着树枝使劲摇晃起来,摇晃了大半天,也没见摇下一个菱角。他一边摇树枝,一边奇怪地自言自语:"这么大一棵树,怎么只长了一个?"

90. Looking for Water Chestnuts

A man living in the mountains came to a riverbank and took a rest under a tree. Noticing there was a water chestnut under the tree, he picked it up and tried to eat it. He found it sweet and floury, very pleasant to the taste. So he climbed up the tree, pulled the branches and shook them as hard as he could. But even after a long while not a single water chestnut fell down. He murmured, quite puzzled, as he worked on the branches: "How come there is only one growing on such a big tree?"

---

① 菱角:水生草本植物,叶子浮在水面,果实长在水下,外面的硬壳有角,果肉可以吃。Water chestnut.
② 扳:拨动,扭动。Pull.

216

91. 小懒汉拜师

有个小懒汉,已经懒得十里八乡①出了名,但他觉得自己还没有懒到家②,便提着一块肉,来到一个老懒汉家,想拜这个老懒汉为师,再跟他学几手③。

老懒汉见小懒汉提着肉拜自己为师,心里很高兴,于是指着墙角的案板④对小懒汉说:"你把案板搬过来,我先炒碗菜招待招待你。"

小懒汉一听,眨了眨眼睛说:"师傅,别麻烦了,用案板还得花力气搬。你要是切菜剁⑤肉,尽管在我肚皮上切和剁好了。"

老懒汉见他懒得够水平,配做自己的徒弟,于是高高兴兴地收下了他。

---

① 十里八乡:泛指附近许多地方。Nearby regions.
② 到家:达到相当高的程度或标准。Reach a very high level.
③ 几手:几种、几样技艺。Some skills.
④ 案板:指架起来的砧板。Cutting board.
⑤ 剁:用刀向下砍。Chop.

91. A Lazy Boy Seeks a Master

There was once a boy well known in the local area for his idleness. But he still felt that he was not comfortably lazy enough. So he went to an old lazybones' home, taking a piece of meat with him for the purpose of learning a few tricks from him.

Learning that the lazy boy wanted to become his apprentice, the old lazybones was very pleased, especially with the meat. So he said to the lazy boy, pointing at a chopping board in the corner: "Bring that board here. I'll make a tasty dish for you first."

The lazy boy blinked and said, "Please don't bother with the board, sir, since it will take so much effort to carry it. If you want to chop some meat or vegetables, just do it here on my belly."

The old lazybones thought the boy was really lazy enough to be his apprentice, so he accepted him with delight.

92. 让小偷关门

从前有个小偷，某天夜里到一户人家去偷东西。他进屋摸了大半天，没有发现有什么东西可偷，只好打开门朝外走。

小偷刚迈出门槛，主人便在床上大声喊道："那汉子，你给我关上门再走！"

小偷回过头来，没好气地说："你怎么这样懒，难怪你家里什么东西也没有！"

主人躺在床上，颇为得意地冲着小偷说："你巴不得①我勤快，好挣②下东西给你偷！"

92. Asking a Thief to Close the Door

A thief broke into someone's house one night. After probing around for quite a while he couldn't find anything worth stealing, so he decided to leave.

Just as the thief was crossing the threshold, the owner of the house shouted from his bed: "Hey, close the door before you leave!"

The thief looked back and said peevishly: "How lazy you are! No wonder you've got nothing at home."

The owner, still lying in bed, said triumphantly: "I suppose you wish that I worked hard so that I could buy things for you to steal!"

---

① 巴不得：急切盼望。Eagerly looking forward to.
② 挣：用劳动换取。Earn.

93. 放火三天

从前有个州官叫田登,他的名字要人避讳①。谁要是一不留心用了"登"字,他就大发雷霆⑩,准得打你几十大板。因此全州的人都时时提心③,处处吊胆④。为避免犯讳挨打,当时举州上下不仅不敢用"登"字,甚至连与"登"同音的"灯"也都改读或改写成"火"。

有一年元宵节⑤,准备在州的首府所在地大闹花灯,并准许全州百姓前来游玩观赏。州衙里将为此事通告全州,便写了一些告示张贴到大街小巷。那告示上这样写道:

"本州依照惯例,放火三天!"

---

① 避讳:不愿说出或听到某些会引起不愉快的字眼儿。Taboo.
② 大发雷霆:比喻大发脾气,高声训斥。Furiously.
③ 提心:担心。Worried.
④ 吊胆:害怕。Scared.
⑤ 元宵节:农历正月十五,传统节日,有观灯风俗。The traditional Lantern Festival, falling on the 15th day of the first month by the lunar calendar.

223

93. On Fire for Three Days

Once there was a prefectural governor named Tian Deng. What he hated most was to hear people mention his name. Whoever, by a slip of the tongue, said "Deng" would be whipped. The local people were always on tenterhooks, and to avoid violating the taboo no one dared to say "Deng". As a result, even the word lamp, which had the same sound, had to be written or read as "fire".

One year a grand celebration for the Lantern Festival was to be held in the prefectural capital and all the people were permitted to join the fun. To let people know about it, the prefectural government put up notices along the streets and lanes which read:

"According to traditional custom, this prefecture will be on fire for three days."

94. 省得黄雀拆了对

　　有一次,苏东坡①到一个朋友家去赴宴。筵席上的头一道菜是四只烤黄雀。其中有个客人不管

　　① 苏东坡:(1037－1101):即苏轼,号东坡居士,北宋文学家、书画家。Su Shi, also known as Su Dongpo, a famous poet, painter and calligrapher of the Northern Song Dynasty.

三七二十一①,拿起筷子就连着吃了三只,然后用筷子指着盘子里剩下的一只,对苏东坡说:"您把这只吃了吧?"

苏东坡笑着回答说:"再请! 再请! 省得黄雀拆了对!"

94. Keeping the Sparrows in Pairs

Once Su Dongpo went for dinner at a friend's home. The first course served was four baked sparrows. One of the guests picked up his chopsticks and ate three of them at one go impulsively. Then, pointing to the last one, he said to Su Songpo:"Please partake of that one."

Su Dongpo answered with a smile:"Oh, no. You have it, please. Otherwise they can not pair off."

---

① 不管三七二十一:指不顾利害得失或不问是非情由。Recklessly.

95. "旧爹"与"新爹"

某书生①的父亲名叫阿谷。为了避讳,他读书读到"谷"字时,都要改读为"爹"。

有一次,他读《四书》②,当读到"旧谷既没,新谷已登"时改"谷"为"爹",于是念成"旧爹既没,新爹已登。"同窗听见后,无不哈哈大笑。

---

① 书生:指读书人。Student,scholar.
② 《四书》:指《大学》、《中庸》、《论语》、《孟子》四种儒家经典。
The Four Books:*The Great Learning*,*The Doctrine of the Mean*,*Analects of Confucius*,and *Mencius*.

95. "Old Dad" and "New Dad"

A student's father was called Ah Gu. To avoid pronouncing the word "Gu" (millet) as a taboo out of respect for his father, he always changed "Gu" to "dad" in his reading.

Once he was reading from one of the Four Books: "The old millet is gone, and the new millet has appeared." He changed the lines out of habit to "The old dad is gone, and the new dad has appeared," and the whole class roared with laughter.

96. 从狗洞里进出

从前有个人叫张吴兴,小时候就聪明超群。

他八岁那年,掉了两颗门牙。一个有钱有势的乡绅①见到后,取笑他说:"哎呀!你嘴里为什么开了两个狗洞?"

张吴兴早就恨透了这个乡绅,便应声回答说:"正是为了你好从这里出出进进!"

---

① 乡绅:旧时乡间的有钱有势的绅士。A country squire.

96. Using the Dog's Holes

A man called Zhang Wuxing had always been very clever.

When he was eight years old he lost two front teeth. When the local squire saw this, he made a fun of the boy, saying, "Oh my goodness, why have you opened two dog's holes in your mouth?"

Zhang Wuxing, who had long disliked this man, replied, "For you to go in and out!"

97. 三拐杖

一个姑娘向老大爷问路:"喂,老头儿,往张村去还有多远?"

姑娘连问三次,老大爷才回答说:"三拐杖。"

姑娘奇怪了："路途远近应论①里嘛，怎么论拐杖呀？"

老大爷说："论'理'②你就该叫我一声'老大爷'。你不知礼，我才拿拐杖教训你！"

97. Three Strokes of the Walking Stick

A girl asked an elderly man："Hey，old man，how far is it to Zhang Village？"The girl asked three times before the elderly man answered，"Three strokes of the walking stick."

The girl was puzzled："A road is measure by *li*. Why do you measure it by strokes of a walking stick？"

The old man replied，"You should measure your words and politely call me 'Grandpa'. Since you're so impolite，I'll teach you with my walking stick！"

---

① 论：按照。According to.
② 理：道理，与"里"谐音。Reason. A homophone of 里，*li*，half a km.

98. 回报

　　财主因一笔生意蚀本,痛不欲生①想自尽②,便找出一条很结实的绳子,悬在房梁上,吊了起来。正当财主双脚悬空的时候,仆人进来了,忙剪断了绳子,把他救了下来。在仆人的开导下,财主终于放弃

---

　　① 痛不欲生:悲痛得不想活下去。形容伤心之至。Feel that it is too painful to live.
　　② 自尽:自己结束生命,自杀。To commit suicide.

了轻生①的念头。到了月底,仆人发现自己的工钱比以往少了一吊②钱,便去向财主询问。财主说:"那天你剪断的那根绳子正好值一吊钱。"

98. Repaying a Debt

A rich man was extremely sad because he had suffered a heavy loss in business, so he wanted to take his own life. He found a very strong rope and tied it to a beam in his house. The moment he hung himself, his servant came in. The servant swiftly cut the rope and saved his master. Then he persuaded him to give up the idea of suicide.

At the end of the month the servant found that he had one string of cash less in his pay, so he went to ask his master about this. The rich man said, "The rope you cut the other day was worth exactly one string of cash."

---

① 轻生:不重视自己的生命。多指自杀。Suicide.
② 吊:旧时钱币单位。String of cash.

99. 打着灯笼也难找

有个先生，只学会"赵钱孙李"四个姓氏①却去教书了。他教得很仔细，一个字要教好多日子。学生和家长催他："先生，往下讲吧。"先生说："不急，不急！贪多嚼不烂，一口吃不成胖子。"家长们犯②了猜疑，怀疑这位先生是不学无术的骗子。先生害怕了，领了工资，吃了晚饭，摸黑③逃跑了。家长们发现受了骗，提着灯笼，边追边喊，要把他抓回来。先生闻风丧胆④，一头钻进草垛。家长们打着灯笼找不到，自认倒霉，骂骂咧咧⑤回家了。

不久，这位先生又想去别村教书混饭吃。人家问他："先生的学问怎么样啊？"他回答说："我以前教过书，后来不干了，他们还打着灯笼找我哩！"

---

① 姓氏：表示家族的字，就是姓。Surname.
② 犯：发作，发生。Have; come under (suspicion).
③ 摸黑：在黑暗中摸索。Probe in the dark.
④ 闻风丧胆：一听到风声，就吓破了胆。形容非常害怕。Become panic-stricken even at the sound of wind.
⑤ 骂骂咧咧：指在说话中夹杂着骂人的话。Curse.

236

99. Can't Be Found
Even With a Lamp

A man set himself up as a teacher right after he had learned only the first four characters in a primer. He seemed so meticulous at work that it took several days for him to teach only one character. The pupils and their parents all wanted him to go on to the next character, but he said, "There's no hurry. Don't bite off more than you can chew or expect to become fat after just one meal."

The parents became suspicious that this so-called teacher might be a cheat who had neither learning nor skill. The man, afraid of being found out, took his salary one night after dinner and fled.

When the pupils' parents found out, they chased after him, carrying lamps and shouting loudly. The man was so panic-stricken by the shouts that he squeezed into a haystack. The parents could not find him even with the help of the lamps. They cursed the man and their bad luck all the way home.

Before long, the man tried again to get a job as a teacher in another village. People there asked him: "How's your learning?" He replied, "I used to teach but I quit later. My pupils' parents were so anxious to have me back that they even took lamps and looked for me at night!"

责任编辑：蔡希勤　　封面设计：李法明

图书在版编目（CIP）数据

中国历代笑话精选(3):汉英对照/陈懿编.-北京：华语教学出版社，1997.7

ISBN 7-80052-509-0

I. 中... II. 陈...III. ①对外汉语教学-语言读物，笑话-汉、英 ②笑话-中国-对照读物-汉、英 IV.H195.5

中国版本图书馆 CIP 数据核字（1997）第 04121 号

中国历代笑话精选（三）

陈　懿　编注　于　岑　翻译

*

©华语教学出版社

华语教学出版社出版

（中国北京百万庄路 24 号）

邮政编码　100037

电话：(86) 10-68995871 / 68326333

传真：(86) 10-68326333

电子信箱：sinolingua@ihw.com.cn

北京外文印刷厂印刷

中国国际图书贸易总公司发行

（中国北京车公庄西路 35 号）

北京邮政信箱第 399 号　邮政编码 100044

新华书店国内发行

1997 年（40 开）第一版

2002 年第三次印刷

（汉英）

ISBN 7-80052-509-0 / H · 686（外）

定价：10.00 元

9－CE－2594PC